Boost your
Mind
&
ImmuneSystem

Sonja Flandorfer

Austria's "Coolest" Lady

The Power of
Mind Management
& Cold Therapy

Commitment & Trust – Your Path to
a Happier and Healthier Life

www.keep-on-cooling.com

The Power of Mind Management
& Cold Therapy
Commitment & Trust –
Your Path to a Happier and Healthier Life
2nd Edition 2021
1st Edition 2020
© by Sonja Flandorfer
Esterhazyweg 3
2491 Neufeld

Contact: info@keep-on-cooling.com

Cover design:
KaDo, Dominika Kalcher, www.kado.co.at
Photo of Sonja Flandorfer on the back cover:
Andrea Peller
Translated by Cynthia Pecking, cynthiapecking@gmail.com

Contents

Foreword by Prof. Dr. Manfred Winterheller.............. 8

Preface from the Author 11

1. Lymphatic Cancer and the Rolling Stones 15

2. When the Two WHs (*Winterheller* and *Wim Hof*) Came Into my Life... 21

3. Freelancing and its Pitfalls 46

4. My Training to Become a Wim Hof Instructor........ 78

5. Control is Good – Trust is Better. The Cold is Your Best Teacher 92

6. Breathe Yourself to Freedom 103

6.1. Practical example.. 110

7. Poland, Wim Hof Winter Travel, February 2020 .. 115

8. Society, Prejudices and Morning Routines........... 122

8.1 Morning routines and all that jazz................. 131

8.2. Prejudices about cold therapy..................... 137

8.3. Implementation into everyday life 143

9. Your Commitment and the Reaction of Others.... 147

10. Practical Examples of Determination, Action and Trust.. 152

10.1. Example 1 – Trust yourself 152

10.2. Example 2 - Trust your body.................. 155

10.3. Example 3 - Trust your gut 158

11. Summary and Tips 161

11.1. Clarifying action, commitment and trust 164

11.2. The best way to use ToDo lists 166

11.3. Goalify – An app to keep you on track 167

Book Tips 172

Acknowledgments 175

Annex... 177

Foreword by
Prof. Dr. Manfred Winterheller

Shoulda, coulda, woulda
are the last words of a fool.
(Beverley Knight)

Shoulda, coulda, woulda are words that run like a central thread through most people's lives. Of course, no one would admit to that themselves.

It feels like we're constantly making decisions, and if you set the bar too low for the decisions you make, then shoulda, coulda, woulda becomes your reality. In the morning, we choose between coffee or tea, but in theory, we could also skip both altogether. We decide that today's not the day to quit smoking, but in reality, we could in fact quit today. We make the choice to drive to work and—like every day—to take the car, but theoretically, we could actually walk to work today or take the bus, or really, we could just quit our job altogether.

But are those really decisions? Or are we just stereotypically obeying the habits in our brain? Choosing to ignore our usual impulses and skip the coffee or actually make today the day we stop smoking, or to finally get more active or even go as far as to pursue the long-time wish of changing careers... those would definitely constitute decisions, even hard ones. And that's what makes them so rare.

Sonja Flandorfer is one of these impressive, extraordinary examples. She shares her journey with us, how she deals with inner resistance and how she makes decisions that force her out of her comfort zone and show her something unexpected: her own life portrait.

She describes this in such an open, authentic and, at the same time, exciting way, that she gives us the courage to dare to do the same.

These are not temporary decisions, likes ones made on a whim at a hotel bar, but decisions that take the reader on a journey of discovery of numerous, courageous and far-reaching choices, unlike the ones that fade away along with a high blood alcohol level. Sonja Flandorfer makes the conscious decision that it can only be called a decision if she actually goes through with it. She doesn't just make an honest attempt, only to back out at the first sign of a challenge. No, she knows that true commitment is the only thing that brings about change.

She calls this 'seeing something through' and thus describes one of the key skills of successful people. Persistence, the ability to see something through, even when it's difficult and draining, is much more effective than a high IQ.

The fact that she adds that we have to learn to trust, instead of overthinking everything to pieces, proves that she knows her stuff. As long as we continue to believe that we can understand everything, plan everything, and break through any barrier with our intellect, we haven't actually comprehended a thing. Wisdom doesn't come from thinking. Thinking leads to inner noise. Only through inner silence and inner attentiveness can action arise that creates harmony with everything around us and anchors us in the here and now.

What sounds like a life philosophy that might suit a few gurus somewhere out in the icy caves of the Himalayas actually turns out to be quite practical and a precondition, a must have, for real success.

Sonja Flandorfer calls this trust. Steve Jobs once said that when we look forward, all we can do is trust. And the wise say that once we learn to trust, the quiet voices that are there to guide us begin to softly speak.

If you want to treat yourself to something good, then read this book. It is short and to the point, without the detours and without the fillers. It will enrich your life and will not leave you disappointed.

Love, Manfred Winterheller

Preface from the Author

Anyone who read my first book knows what's coming. A typical marker of my books: I love smileys. I'm not concerned (nor have I ever been) with whether or not that's something I should or shouldn't do, or whether or not people like it. ☺

So what compelled me to write another book? After releasing my book *Glücklich für immer? So a Schaß!* [original title] in 2018, I received a lot of positive feedback. Readers could relate, and had found themselves in similar situations. They asked me: "So what happened in your life after 2016 (the year I finished my first book)? How did you get to where you are today?"

And yes, it really is a story worth telling, because it's fascinating to see how my life developed as a whole and how situations and experiences were intricately woven together. It's extraordinary what can happen when you decide to do three things:

Make decisions,
take action
and trust!

And that's what this book is about. It's actually about a lot more than making simple decisions; it's about deciding to do something and committing yourself to making it happen. It's about commitment and trust. Those two words will accompany us through the entire book.

Commitment! Trust!

I am writing this book in alignment with who I am. With authenticity, and in whatever direction the wind blows me. It might not be textbook perfect. But that makes it approachable and easy to understand, and much more full of life. There will be passages where you'll know what I mean. 😊

I will tell you a lot about my own life in this book. Why? Because it's the only life where I've had a constant front-row seat. 😊

I hope that you'll be able to relate to the various stories, like so many of those who read my first book. That encouraged me to reveal a great deal about myself in this second book. I know how much it helps people. It shows them that they're not alone, that there are others out there who feel the same way. And by telling my story, I might even help YOU find your path to a happier and healthier life. What part of this book can YOU relate to?

Dear reader, this book is designed to help you navigate life with (even) more commitment and (even) more trust.

In particular, I'll be writing about two men who have had a strong influence on my life. This book is therefore also a heartfelt "thank you", from the bottom of my heart, to:

Prof. Dr. Manfred Winterheller

and

Wim Hof, "The Iceman".

Thank you both for coming into my life and for turning it on its head. In the most positive sense, of course. 😊

And a big thank you goes out to all of my friends, relatives and acquaintances who continue to support me and take my crazy ideas seriously.

Life is meant to be fun and to bring us joy.
I believe that with all of my heart.

Now my wish for YOU is that you enjoy reading this book, and that you go on to lead a happy and healthy life. 😊

1. Lymphatic Cancer and the Rolling Stones

06.16.2014

I'm in the hospital; I can't lift my head, and the Rolling Stones are playing at the Ernst Happel Stadium. I've never seen the Stones live, and had bought myself tickets for the special day. They've been on stage for 50 years now. It was so hard to score those tickets. I had to be at my computer when the ticket sales opened, and had to jump as soon as the tickets became available. YES! Got them! Two tickets for the Rolling Stones. 😊

Now I'm not exactly a major Stones fan, but they are a part of music history and I was determined to go to a show—at least once—and to be able to one day tell my grandkids: "I saw them live." Just like my parents bragged to us about how they saw Ike & Tina Turner live. Wow, what I would have given for that experience (yep, that's right, I'm an Ike & Tina Turner fan through and through). 😊

OK, back to the here and now. So I'm not in a stadium packed with thousands of other cheering fans. I'm lying in the hospital with a stitched-up wound on my neck. I can't sleep because my roommate just had nasal surgery and is snoring like a bear. Not exactly how I imagined my first Stones show – a snoring concert!

I've just had a lymph node removed. And it was urgent! For weeks, months even, I've been suffering from swollen lymph nodes, and they were getting bigger and bigger. X-rays, ultrasounds, MRIs... I had every test under the sun.

The doctors couldn't say anything for sure, only one thing: we had to remove the largest lymph node right away before it grew any bigger, and then we'd have to examine it. Suspected case of lymphatic cancer. And no, this surgery couldn't wait until after the Stones concert, because we had to act fast here.

When you're lying in the hospital, eyes wide open, but unable to move your head, and your roommate is snoring, you start to think. What if I really do have cancer? In an effort to cover all my bases, I went ahead and asked Dr. Google what it might be like to have lymphatic cancer. And dear reader, if I may, let me give you one tip at the start of this book: NEVER, NEVER, really... NEVER ask Dr. Google about a medical condition! What you'll read there surpasses pretty much any Hitchcock film from the previous century on the scary scale (to all of my readers under 40: just google "Alfred Hitchcock"). ☺

I started thinking: what if I die? When it comes to lymphatic cancer, that's the most likely scenario. What do I want to do with the time I have left? Do I want to go on living like this? What would I change? And so here comes my second tip: this is something you can also ask yourself when you're *not* lying in the hospital waiting for some test results. Are you living YOUR life? How YOU have imagined it? What would you change about your life, if you only had one year left to live?

**What would you change about your life,
if you only had one year left to live?**

So I'm lying there, reflecting, and I decided it might be a good time to listen to the mp3 files that Alexandra, a coworker, had given me. Alexandra is a really nice lady that I first got to know at work, before becoming good friends in July 2011. Here's how the story goes:

It was a Friday in July of 2011. I was trying to reach a friend who always took care of my cats when I was on vacation. His name was Thomas. I had known him since I was 15. We went to the same dance school in the 1st district in Vienna.

I was trying to reach him to ask if he could take care of my cats again while I was away. I kept calling and calling, wondering why he didn't call back. Then suddenly, someone answered, a man, but it wasn't Thomas. I asked who he was. He said he was a colleague. I asked about Thomas. The man asked who I was. I said: "a friend." "What's your relationship to Thomas?", he asked. I grew impatient and said in a loud, irritated voice: "Listen up, man. I've been trying to reach Thomas for days and I'm running out of time. I'm about to leave on vacation, and wanted to go over the final details with him about my cats." And because I had a gnawing feeling that something wasn't right, I added: "Now please tell me what's going on."

There was a brief silence on the other end of the line. Then his answer: "Thomas is dead." I was floored, and began to stutter: "What? How? What happened? Was he in an accident?" The man hesitated, then got up the nerve and told me the truth: "No, suicide."

Now I was really at a loss for words. I thanked him, hung up and sat there, in total shock. I just sat there. I couldn't bring myself to do anything, not even cry. After what felt like an eternity, it finally hit me. I started crying, and ran into the copy room where I thought I'd be undisturbed... because yes, I was still at the office.

On the way there, I passed Alexandra's office. She noticed right away that something was wrong and came after me. I told her what had happened, at least what I had understood to have happened. In that moment— and still today, by the way—she was a true angel. It wasn't until I got home that I realized that there had been a police operation here in Neufeld last weekend. A helicopter was flying around and everyone was in a flurry of excitement. It never occurred to me back then that the operation had to do with Thomas, that one of my best friends would take his own life. I had known Thomas for over 20 years and would have never suspected anything like that.

Alexandra brought me a USB stick a few days later. She said I should listen to Manfred Winterheller's CDs on the stick, that they would help me a lot. Back then, the name Winterheller meant nothing to me, and I didn't think I had any need for the audio files, but I was very grateful to Alexandra for thinking of me. I put the stick aside and three years later, lying in the hospital with my neck full of stitches, I thought about it again.

Another reason I had never listened to the mp3s was because I didn't know how. And sitting in front of the computer, staring into the oblivion and listening to something was just too boring. But technology and my knowledge of it had improved over the years, so I decided I would listen to the CDs in my car. After all, I did have a two-hour commute to work every day, an hour to work and an hour back.

Six years have passed since then. It's the spring of 2020 – and incidentally, I'm still alive, obviously. ☺

This book is about the past six years. It's about mindset, breathing, cold therapy and most of all, about YOU, and about how you can improve YOUR life.

So what happened back in 2014 in the hospital, and where did it lead? I was diagnosed with "suspected sarcoidosis." OK, so no cancer. That's a good start. But what exactly is sarcoidosis? I ended up consulting Dr. Google again, because the real doctors—with all due respect—weren't really able to explain it to me. They just kept beating around the bush. But I soon understood why. Sarcoidosis is a condition that is so rare, that there is also no cure for it. It can flare up, but it doesn't have to. If it does flare up, you die, but in most cases, there is a spontaneous recovery and it never flares up. Huh?

OK, so here's what I knew: this is a disease that primarily affects the lymph nodes and the lungs, and the doctors told me that if I ever have a serious cough over a long period of time, that I should get checked for sarcoidosis. If that's not the case, there's nothing to worry about.

I decided right then and there to just never cough again.

Commitment! Trust!

At the time, it wasn't clear to me how much that decision affected me at a subconscious level. Today I know how much influence a decision like that can have. And in case you're wondering, I've only had one cough since then, and I managed to get rid of it in two days with a good dose of commitment and trust. 😊

2. When the Two WHs (*W*inter*h*eller and *W*im *H*of) Came Into my Life

After going back to work in June 2014 following my operation and the more or less positive outcome, I began listening to the mp3s from Alexandra on my commute. Wow, what Manfred Winterheller had to say made a lot of sense. He had a *different* way of thinking, a bit weird in fact, but it all made sense. As an overthinker, logic was very important to me. I had a hard time with hocus-pocus. I immediately tried a few things out, such as not always having to be right. As a former schoolteacher, that was a hard one. ☺

I wanted to know more about him and started looking for books. I decided that a seminar would be even better. OK, great, there's one scheduled in November 2014. Whaaaaat? No way. The six-day seminar in Kitzbühel costs € 2,490? And hotel and meals are not included? He's crazy! Well, lunch was obviously included. That's at least something. ☺

No way, I'm definitely not going at that price. Forget it. I talked to Alexandra about Winterheller. She told me that a friend of hers went to the seminar and said it was phenomenal. She said she went to a one-day seminar and loved it. I was so torn. I had two voices in my head.

The first one said: "Go for it. No risk, no fun. What's going to happen? If you like the CDs so much, think about what the six-day seminar will be like."

The other voice said: "That's a total rip-off. If he's really that good and wants to make a change in the world, he should offer it for less money. He just wants to get rich; he doesn't care about helping people." With both of those voices in my head, 2014 came to an end and I still hadn't signed up for the seminar.

But after less than a year, I had made so many small, super positive steps in my life simply by following the tips on the CDs that I decided to go to Kitzbühel in November of 2015. No matter what it costs!

Commitment! Trust!

I turned 40 in August of 2015 and asked for money for Manfred Winterheller's Mind Management seminar, to take place in November.

The seminar lasted from noon on Thursday to noon on Tuesday, for six hours each day. My husband went with me but did not attend the seminar. He spent his time taking walks and exploring Kitzbühel.

We would meet up at lunch and in the evening and I would talk a mile a minute, rattling off everything I had just learned. At some point it all became too *spooky* for him and on Sunday, he decided to go home because he understood absolutely nothing I was talking about.

I don't want to go into any more detail here about the seminar either, because it's quite simply not the topic of this book, BUT, and this is very important to say: the seminar changed my life forever, and took me in many new directions. For this book, I would like to single out just one small part of the seminar. In fact, it was so small that I had no idea that it would go on to determine my entire life today.

It's about Wim Hof!

Manfred Winterheller showed us a commercial for a company that makes heated jackets. In the clip, Wim jumps into an ice hole, swims a long distance under thick ice and emerges from another hole. Then he runs over to a glass box, gets in and two men fill it with ice cubes. Next to him, there is a man fully dressed in a heated jacket. The speaker says: "Sure, you can use the power of your mind to stay warm, but this electric heated jacket might just keep you even warmer."

It was pretty clear what the commercial had triggered in me: I *had to have* that awesome heated jacket. I needed it! Because I didn't believe for a second that you can use the power of your mind to stay warm. I wondered why Manfred Winterheller showed us that example, because everything else he had said was inspiring, logical, understandable and, above all, possible with a little practice. But "using your mind to stay warm," well, that was a little too far-fetched for me.

After the seminar, I didn't give it any more thought. I implemented a lot of the other things I had heard and learned and that was more than enough to keep me busy.

Even if it sounds like something trivial, I treated myself to my dream hairstyle right after the seminar. I had dark, shoulder-length hair and two weeks later I was sporting a blond, short, spiky haircut, which is now my trademark. How often people say: "Sonja Flandorfer… is that the little lady with the short, blond hair? The cold-therapy gal?" ☺

At the time, of course, I didn't know that my short, blond (or rather grayish) hair and cold therapy would become my trademarks.

After the seminar in November 2015, I also decided to give a presentation at my company on some of the topics I had learned in this life-changing seminar.

And that was really wild. Like crazy wild, absolutely out of the norm. Why? Because I was an assistant, a "lobby plant", as my mother used to say. ☺ In other words, there's the mighty boss and then there's me, the person you have to pass to get to him.

I've been a lot of things in my life. A deputy branch manager in a supermarket, an invoicing clerk, a secretary and a high school math, physics and chemistry teacher. I used to teach tennis, and now, I was an assistant. I even had other jobs in between, but there are too many to list. ☺

I hardly ever stuck with a job for more than two years. I always got bored when the challenge faded away. I was always interested in learning and growing. I stayed at my last company the longest, a full 7.5 years, changing positions several times within the company. In 2015, when I attended Manfred Winterheller's Mind Management seminar, I was working as the assistant to the Argentinean Alejandro Plater, the CEO of Telekom Austria at the time. It was an exciting job with an exciting boss.

What made him so different from my Austrian bosses, for example, was the fact that he was always looking for solutions to problems, not for someone to blame. That was something, and still is today, that many people in the company couldn't understand. ☺

But let's get back to the Winterheller seminar and what came out of it. I came back and told Alejandro that I wanted to give a lecture in the A1 auditorium (an in-house auditorium) about what I had learned. He got a big smile on his face, and said: "If you want to do that, then go for it." He was even a bit surprised I had asked for his approval. He believes that if someone wants to do something and their heart is really in it, they should do it. Wow. I was impressed. From that point on, it would take another three months to get there, with an enormous number of hurdles...

It all played out in exactly the way he had said it would in the seminar. "If you start to change, most people won't know how to handle it because you no longer conform to the 'system.' So be confident in your decision and see it through. The best thing you can do is to not talk about it at all, only with people who truly support you."

Done. I shared my idea with a handful of people I trusted, including my husband Josef, Alexandra, my coworker who gave me the Winterheller mp3s, Carina from Communications and Erich, who was responsible for technology in the A1 auditorium. Now I could tell you a lot about each and every one of these wonderful people, but I'll use Erich as an example.

The seminar taught me that when you are determined and committed, when you go for something with all your might and believe in it with all your heart, then life lines up and things start to happen that you would never have expected.

**When you go for something with all your might and
believe in it with all your heart,
then life lines up and things start to happen
that you would never have expected.**

Doors begin to open that weren't even there before. You get to know people that you didn't know before and you get to know other people who you already knew, on a much deeper level.

Erich belonged to that second group of people. A nice guy who I always liked, always friendly, always helpful, but not someone I knew well. I called him on December 23, 2015 at lunchtime. Again, to be clear, it was December 23rd!! One day before Christmas Eve. I asked him if he could let me into the A1 auditorium, just for a quick five minutes. I wanted to stand on the stage and see how I felt there, to get a feel for whether the stage is something for me. He was really nice and supportive and said he'd be happy to let me in, but that it would have to wait until 4 p.m. because it was still being used.

I went down to the auditorium at 4 p.m. and Erich was waiting for me. I went up on stage... for the first time in my life. That feeling – it was indescribable. I loved being on stage. In that very moment, I thought to myself, "YES, this is what I want. I want to be on stage."

Erich disappeared and suddenly the lights in the auditorium switched off. The stage lights came on and I was standing under a sea of brilliant spotlights directed right at me. He sat down in the auditorium and looked up at me. He told me I could begin.

I rambled off a bunch of stuff and asked him how my presence was on stage. He said: "Great." He suddenly got up again, went into some back room and emerged two minutes later with a headset. He wired me up, went to his sound board, turned up the sound and said: "Now say what you want to say to the people." I was caught off guard. I hadn't prepared any text, so I babbled off something. He laughed and said that there were plenty of senior managers who wouldn't have done any better, even though they're often on stage and earn five times as much. I should just go for it.

Erich took a total of two hours for me that day, which we spent in the auditorium, experimenting and talking. Wow, what a guy. He stayed there until 6 p.m. on December 23rd, simply because Sonja had got it in her head that she would give a lecture to a crowd of people in the A1 auditorium, although she had never done that before.

How many other people would have laughed at me? Talked me out of it? How many people would have said: "Sonja, stick with what you know." or "You do realize you're just an assistant, right?" But Erich had my back.

He gave me honest feedback and encouragement. Erich, I'll never forget it.

The voices of opposition would come from somewhere else. And of course, I was bound to hear this: "What if every employee suddenly starts doing this?" What these "what if everyone does it" people unfortunately hadn't considered, is that it's never the case that *everyone* does it. And if a few do it, well, that's great. Leading up to March 17, 2016, the day of the lecture, there were countless hurdles to overcome. So many of them!

There were also tons of things that forced me to *break the rules*, as Arnold Schwarzenegger said in his famous speech "The Six Rules of Success." If you want to achieve something, you have to escape your old habits and break some rules. Schwarzenegger himself says that this doesn't mean you should break any laws, but that you have to keep redefining the limits and the rules if you want to do something outside the norm.

And you need people who have your back. That's where Erich comes in again. At the Mind Management seminar I learned a lot, but one important thing I learned was this: "Luck is when preparation meets opportunity, and there's always opportunity. So be prepared." So I knew that to be ready for my lecture, I had to practice, practice, practice, practice. But there's a difference between practicing in front of your dog in your living room or directly in the auditorium with a few people in *live mode*.

So, it was time to *break the rules*. My groupies and I spent our evenings rehearsing in the A1 auditorium, once the company had emptied out for the day. Erich was always there to set things up. They sacrificed their free time to help me achieve my dream. As I write this, I am full of gratitude. 😊

On March 17, 2016, the day had come. My first lecture, in front of 200 people. Half of them came because they liked me, because they were eager to see the outcome, and because they wanted to support me. The other half came because they were curious, and some came because they wanted to see me fail. "Sonja thinks she's better than us, just because she's the assistant to the CEO. Now she's giving lectures."

The mix of energy was palpable in there, but I stuck to what I had learned in Prof. Dr. Manfred Winterheller's seminar. No more scanning your notes before the performance. Just blast some motivating music, loosen up those shoulders, drop into a power pose and embrace a feeling of positivity. And that's exactly what I did.

Commitment! Trust!

I took to the stage. Applause. I started to speak, and after three sentences the first fumble... Ahhhhhh! But I recovered quickly and when I was finished, I still can hardly believe it today: a standing ovation.

It was magical, paralyzing... people were lined up to talk to me afterwards. I was sure of one thing that night: while it might sound strange to many of you, I knew that it wasn't me speaking that night, but that someone was speaking through me.

After the lecture, I couldn't remember a thing. Not one word. Nothing. Even during the lecture, I didn't think about what I was saying. I just spoke, or someone spoke through me. Today I know what that is. It's called *flow*. I was over the moon.

The feedback on the company's intranet over the next few days was spectacular. It even went so far that my coworkers were demanding an encore. Some who had heard how great it was apologized for not having time to see it, and asked if I could do it again.

Can you imagine my reaction? Total fright! Paralyzing fear! Why? It makes sense really... I did it well once, but what if I failed the second time around? What if I couldn't meet everyone's expectations, which were now so high?

Have you ever felt like that? How often have you been asked to do something, and you don't know if you can live up to the expectations? And then there's the typical core beliefs: "I'm not good enough." "Maybe it was just beginner's luck." "What if I make a fool of myself?"

Everything I had learned in Winterheller's seminar was suddenly gone. Out the window. So much for Commitment and Trust! All that was left was fear.

I called a meeting with my *core team*, laid my fears out on the table, and what did they do? They recited back to me EXACTLY what I had said on stage. What about "practice, practice, practice" and "never give up?" They said I should listen to my own lecture. Everyone is motivated as hell now, except for me. I should practice what I preach, put my own advice into action. Damn it! They got me! OK, back to the drawing board.

It was time to binge on the Manfred Winterheller mp3s again, skim through my seminar notes, look back over everything and find my spirit. It took me a month, but then I was sure... I'm doing it! On June 7, 2016, I gave the lecture again.

A lot had happened professionally in those two months leading up to June 2016. But before I go into that, let me tell you about the second lecture. I practiced and practiced; I was motivated, but scared too. Do you know that fear of the second time? You did something really well once and now you have to deliver again? But the more I practiced, the more confident I became.

This time, there was a great turnout and it was just as well received as the first time. Whew... lucky break. 🙂 Or was it? Don't forget: luck is when preparation meets opportunity, so be prepared. The moral of the story? Practice!

But back to what happened in the two months leading up to the second lecture... I wanted to switch to the HR department because I was interested in helping people more and wanted to get rid of my *assistant stamp*. At the company, it went something like this: "Once an assistant, always an assistant," and you were totally underestimated. Alejandro thought a move to HR would be good for me and was supportive of my drive to learn and grow, even if it meant he had to do without a great assistant himself.

In the meantime, specifically on May 1, 2016, Margarete Schramböck, who is now the Minister of Digital and Economic Affairs in Austria, became the CEO of A1 Telekom Austria AG. Before I switched to HR, I trained my successor and Margarete's assistant at the same time. I loved this *limbo period* because I was able to pass on my knowledge, which was precisely what I wanted to do, pass on my knowledge.

But when I started in HR, I wasn't able to do what I wanted to do. I was assigned ancillary duties. I approached the department manager at the time with a concept, but she didn't even really listen to me. I realized pretty quickly that HR is not about the people; it's not about the employees, but about winning some sort of Change Awards, generating statistics and surveys and achieving a state of self-celebration.

It *was* actually about the employees as a resource, but not about the people themselves. I was disappointed. And angry with myself for not understanding this earlier. I was annoyed with how naive I had been.

The HR department needed an employee who would carry out orders, not someone who has a mind of her own and wants to see people grow. But that's what I wanted to do, with all my heart. But *hearts* had no business there.

After dragging myself to work every day with an upset stomach and deciding that I was *done*, because I was already at the point of burnout (see my first book *Glücklich für immer? So a Schaß!* [original title]), and because I was already familiar with the feeling that was bubbling up inside of me, I decided one morning to do something I had never done before. I stayed home and called in sick, even though I wasn't sick at all. Although, that's not entirely true, I felt sick as soon as I thought of going to work. I cried, was in total despair and didn't know which way to turn. I had no idea what to do.

Out of nowhere, I got a Whatsapp from my coworker, my friend, Sabine. We shared an office at work back then. She sent me an excerpt from the book *The Secret*, without knowing that it would change my life for good. I can't remember which passage it was, but I can tell you one thing: "I read it and KNEW exactly what to do." I quit!

I was done with that company, done being told what to do. I finally want to do what I enjoy, helping people, being there for others, motivating them to find their power. I'M GOING TO BE A FREELANCE SPEAKER! That feeling was strong, and it was good. I couldn't imagine working at that company for one more day.

It was an impulse. I can't describe it, but it came from *somewhere*. Today I would say that *The Force* spoke to me and gave me the feeling. Back then all I knew was that it felt right.

Getting my husband on board that night was a bit harder.

But: **Commitment. Trust.**

We talked far into the night. We had a blunt conversation about the consequences of giving up a safe job with a secure income to pursue an uncertain future with no idea what it will bring. We talked about success and failure. But I was so determined to never take orders again that we decided that evening we would accomplish it as a team. At this point, thank you again to my wonderful husband. 😊

The very next day I took the necessary steps and what happened next was unbelievable. I heard it all. People who said: "Are you crazy? You're giving up all of this for a completely uncertain future?" Then there were others who said: "Wow, I admire you. I wouldn't be brave enough to do it, but I wish you the best of luck." Then there were those who said: "That's right, Sonja! Don't let people tell you what to do. Blaze your own trail. And when you're a success, I'll do it too." Huh?

And then of course there were all the amazing people I had met in the past few years since beginning my work with mind management. They said: "You can do it! I believe in you. If you need anything, I'm here for you." Those were exactly the type of people I wanted to attract into my life going forward. Positive, motivating people who don't go through life with their blinkers on. People who move out of their comfort zone, dare to try new things and trust in themselves. People who are ready to fail but to jump back on the horse, who support others and are not too proud to ask for help.

People with esteem, who treat other people with respect and know what respect means. Those are the type of people I love. Today, it's a wonderful spring day in 2020 and I can say that 95% of the time, I'm surrounded by precisely those types of people. 😊

So I started working on my own business in July 2016. My vision: "Tu, felix Austria." A vision where every single Austrian would lead a self-determined, happy, healthy life. Since I know that self-determination, self-confidence, trust in the future and trust in something bigger are the key components to happiness, I wanted everyone to know and implement it, with the goal of helping people find happiness.

Naive? Perhaps! But maybe not. I don't know if you read my last book, but it paints a clear picture of how I played the victim role. Thirty years of my life as a victim. But from that point on, that started to change slowly but surely. Today I know that if you play the victim, you let others determine your life. You give other people power over you, power over your life, your thoughts and your actions. Why is that? Because a lot of times, we just want to function, to belong and to live a *normal* life. What more can we expect from life?

I now know that there is another way to be happy and that is the purpose of this book. To show you that if I, the super victim, have managed to take my life into my own hands, then YOU can do it too. I know that for sure!

OK, OK, so we don't know each other. You might be thinking, "Well, if you knew, Sonja, what MY life is really like, you wouldn't be so sure." You know what? You're right! I don't know you! But I don't need to either, because now, after working with so many people, I know really well what people are like. I don't mean to say that everyone is the same, but there is a common thread that runs through most people's lives, and it's this: think too much, trust too little.

**People think too much
and trust too little!**

Most people want to have control over their life, to make plans and to always know in advance what's going to happen. Listen up all you overthinkers: it won't work!

Go to YouTube and put this in: "Steve Jobs, Connecting the Dots." Total motivation and passion.

In his speech, he says very clearly—and Steve Jobs was one of the most successful people of all time—"You can't connect the dots looking forward; you can only connect them looking backwards. So you have to trust that the dots will somehow connect in your future. You have to trust in something — your gut, destiny, life, karma, whatever."

I recommend listening to that entire speech. The main message is perfectly clear: it's only in retrospect that we can see why things happened the way they did, and how the events are connected; when we look forward, all we can do is trust.

This passage in the book is one of the most important of all. I sincerely hope that YOU just had an Aha moment. Wim Hof, "The Iceman," uses this approach all the time. He trusts! He truly believes in what he does. He's committed and he trusts.

Commitment! Trust!

By the way, it's not just Wim Hof. There are so many people who live out this principle:

Set goals, so you know where you want to go, and then trust the journey. Sure, you have to know where you're going; otherwise, there's no journey. But even if you know where you want to go, there will always be detours in the road that just pop up, and you should take them.

I'll give you an example from my life, and we'll tie it into the story of my first seminar with Prof. Dr. Manfred Winterheller.

I mentioned that he showed us a commercial for a heated jacket, and in that commercial, that Wim Hof used his mind alone to stay warm. Practically a frigophobic myself, I didn't want anything to do with that. I implemented many of the other things from the seminar, and I practiced trust. When I started to set up my own business in June 2016, I had a clear goal. But how would I get there? I wanted to give lectures and share everything I had learned with people. I was highly motivated. I came up with a company name, "Keep on Goaling", soon had a logo, a website, a number of merchandise items and a lecture entitled "RIGHT NOW!".

In November 2016, I went to Manfred Winterheller's seminar in Kitzbühel again, but this time I took my husband, my daughter and my best friend with me. I felt that it was important for the people around me to understand why I was doing what I was doing, and my friend then decided to work with me to build "Keep on Goaling." We attended seminars, both online and live, and educated ourselves at every level. "Marketing", "How to give a speech", "How to set up a website", "How to upsell", "How to sell effectively", and so on.

Who knows how much information we processed during that time? At this point we were completely in our heads. Everything was meticulously planned. We listened to every expert we could to learn from the best.

I'd like to pick up there again later, but now I'll jump to what I mentioned on the last page, namely that you should seize opportunities when they come into your life.

At the 2016 seminar, Prof. Dr. Manfred Winterheller brought up The Iceman, Wim Hof, once again. My life had changed so much in the previous year, since the 2015 seminar, and I believed so much in what Manfred Winterheller had to say that I still couldn't understand why he kept pushing The Iceman. Can someone please tell me how you're supposed to use your mind, your thinking, to stay warm? When I'm cold, I'm cold. Period. Done. Basta. And when I'm cold, I throw on some clothes. Problem solved!

But since I held Manfred in such high regard, I thought, OK, I'll give it a chance and I googled Wim Hof. I read about 26 world records and hiking in nothing but shorts up a mountain in unbelievable freezing temperatures, etc. OK, I've heard enough. Wim Hof, for me, is nothing but a nut. And I knew one thing for sure, he would certainly never have anything to do with MY life. So I tossed out the topic again and devoted myself to the many other things that I had learned in the seminar.

In July 2017, I flew to see Tony Robbins in New Jersey as part of my training, learning and seminar-addiction mania. "Unleash the Power Within." A huge spectacle, 14,000 people and the guy lit up the room. It was amazing! I was a little disappointed that Tony was only on stage for two of the four days.

On the last day, a Sunday, it felt more like a sales event. Every hour a different speaker came out and talked about what was so extremely fantastic about his or her product. I was about to leave when something inside me said: "Sonja, you're not really going to fly all the way from Austria to America just to skip out on the seminar early, are you? Are you crazy? Stay put." I trusted that voice, as I had learned from Manfred Winterheller, but was a little disgruntled because I wasn't sure why I should stay put when I wasn't going to buy any of those products anyway.

It wasn't too long before I knew why. Wim Hof came out on stage and at that moment, I lost it. I can't describe it with the best of intentions. I started screaming "unbelievable", "unbelievable" and was practically shaking because Wim Hof was up there on stage. When I came back to my senses, I wondered why I had reacted like that. He's nothing but a nut that I want nothing to do with.

But my feeling, this voice—sorry, but I really can't describe it any other way—was shrieking inside of me: "You have to meet him. You have to meet him. Do something. Anything!" I was full of adrenaline and my thoughts were swirling in my head. I was sitting all the way at the top, in the nosebleed section, and it was America, which meant I had absolutely no chance of reaching the speakers. I couldn't even get to the lower part of the auditorium, where I might be able to shout something to Wim like "Photo?". I didn't even know why I wanted to meet him, but I trusted the voice.

I weaseled my way into the lower ranks. That was one of those times where you get creative (break the rules).

☺ But even there, I didn't have a chance of getting noticed. It was an idiotic idea anyway with 14,000 people in there. ☺

OK, Plan B. Wim Hof had to leave the building at some point. He couldn't stay overnight. The building had, hhhmmm... I don't remember, but at least six exits and one exit through the parking garage. I had no idea where he would come out, but I didn't care. As a former running coach with some stellar stamina, I decided to circle the building as many times as possible until he came out of one of the exits.

Now today, I have to laugh at myself because the idea alone was already borderline stupid, or, let's leave the "borderline" out... it was stupid, completely idiotic, because the building was so big that when I was on one side, it took me at least two minutes to get back to the other side and in those two minutes, he could have whisked off in the car so quickly that I wouldn't have even noticed. But the urge inside me was *strong*.

Commitment! Trust!

So I was scurrying past one of the exits when guess what happened next... you can call it what you want, but I call it destiny or fate.

Wim Hof was standing right in front of that exact exit, taking photos with about six people. I stood there, stunned. I couldn't believe it, but I knew one thing right away: life, fate, the universe, the force, or even God—I don't care what you call it—had lined up the stars so that I would meet Wim. Otherwise, it wouldn't have played out the way it did. I talked to him briefly and we took a picture together, which I'm not allowed to print here for legal reasons. I show it at all my workshops, for one very special reason:

What is striking about the photo is how differently we were dressed. 😊 I was wearing four layers, a short-sleeved T-shirt and three long-sleeved vests/a jacket. Wim, well, was in shorts and a T-shirt. This man intrigued me. He was so nice, so authentic, so down-to-earth, so... I have no words. A simply amazing man. I was immediately hooked.

I was fascinated by his aura. I decided then and there to complete his ten-week video course back home in Austria, known as the Fundamentals course.

From that July day in 2017 to December 2018, when I became the only practicing female Wim Hof instructor in Austria, was a long journey, but every second of it paid off. In August 2019, a newspaper called me Austria's "Coolest" Lady. The media began showing an interest in me. What followed were articles in various local newspapers, in the courier, then a radio interview and invitations to speak on podcasts and on television. And that was just the beginning of the journey.

I'm sure I'll write more about that later, but first I'd like to tell you what YOU can get from this example. Here, we have an obvious example of what it means to trust, to listen to your *inner voice*. IN RETROSPECT, I can connect the dots, but before that I would never have dreamed that frigophobe Sonja would one day become a cold therapist. That's not something you can plan! No way! So please, NEVER say that something is impossible or can't be done.

Set a goal, trust in it, blaze your own trail and if a detour suddenly pops up in your life, take notice of it and make it work for you. You may not understand its purpose at first, but that is exactly what it means to TRUST. Trust what life brings you. It all has a reason. It all has a purpose.

Trust what life brings you.
It all has a reason. It all has a purpose.

3. Freelancing and its Pitfalls

As I mentioned in the last chapter, I started my company in July of 2016: Keep on Goaling. One of the ideas behind my company was to make the content I learned from Prof. Dr. Manfred Winterheller accessible to people who couldn't afford € 2,500 for a seminar. I had set a lot of money aside because I knew that if you start your own business, it would likely take a while for it to be profitable. I later learned how spot on that was. I listened to all kinds of motivational, sales, marketing and rhetoric trainers. I completed one seminar after another, took online courses and I studied, studied, studied. I built my company on the side, deciding on a logo and a website and everything that goes with it.

I learned a great deal of things, really a lot, from the whole process:

1. Just because you take courses and collect knowledge doesn't mean that you can put it into practice.
2. Not everything the experts say applies to you. There's not just one path. Most importantly, there is YOUR path, your individual journey.
3. Your own core beliefs play a much bigger role than you think, much more than you will initially want to admit to yourself.

4. Even if all of the seminars preach that mistakes are learning opportunities, you will still get mad every time you make one.
5. If you're a perfectionist like me, Point 4 is a bit harder for you than for others.
6. Don't let people walk all over you. Take action if something doesn't feel right.
7. Learn to lead and then only work with people with whom you want to work.
8. Just because you're good friends doesn't mean you will work well together.
9. But the greatest lesson I learned overall was: LISTEN TO YOUR GUT!

Point 9 wasn't just the greatest lesson I learned, it was also the hardest. I often asked myself: "Does this feel wrong because it really isn't right for me, or because it's new and unknown and I'm afraid to try it?"

It took me a very long time to figure out what my gut instinct even is, or as others would say, what my heart is telling me. I just didn't know whether it might be fear that I was feeling. And even today, I don't always know for sure, but I have at least come up with ways to figure it out.

So what do you have to think about when starting your own business?

1. How should you organize your time?
2. How can you tune out on the weekends?

3. Does going out on your own really mean you're always *on your own*?

4. I've learned so much in my life. Doesn't it make sense to use my skills and education to make a living or put my focus on just one goal?

5. How much sleep do I *really* need?

6. How do I know if I've practiced enough for a speaking engagement?

7. What if this all doesn't turn out like I have imagined it?

8. What if I run out of money before I earn any?

9. Damn it, I really don't want to have to *sell* myself. Why is that so important?

10. I can't afford any employees yet. But they say you should delegate the stuff you don't want to do yourself. How is that supposed to work?

I listened to all the greats. Tony Robbins, Bodo Schäfer, Dirk Kreuter, Christian Bischoff, Brian Tracy and of course, Manfred Winterheller, who for me, however, is not one of the classic greats. He's in a league of his own. He has a totally different approach. The other ones I listed are really similar, which might be due to the fact that everyone has been to see Tony Robbins. I can always recognize when music, phrases and even entire books written by Tony pop up in other seminars.

Sure, Tony Robbins is special, but when I realized that others were just copying him, I was a little disappointed. At first! But when I thought about it some more, I had a revelation! I don't have to reinvent the wheel; it already exists! The only thing that matters is how I sell it! The others didn't come up with anything new either. ☺

I worked really hard on myself and no, it wasn't always a barrel of fun. I can't tell you how many times I've heard from successful people: "If you're working toward your dream, then it won't feel like work. You'll enjoy it." As much as I wanted to believe that—and yes, there were days when I did enjoy it—that wasn't always the case. In fact, that was far too often *not* the case (today, I can say that my work is fun and really brings me joy. I have found the right path).

Back then, I kept trying to find the right path and that was often really tough, but I kept my eye on the goal. But let's look at something positive here: once again, I got to know someone who would go on to play a very important role in my life. I had seen him before, but we had never had anything to do with each other.

In September 2016, I booked a room at the cultural center in Neufeld, my hometown, for March 2017, where I was planning my first public appearance. The person in charge of the center, KUZ Neufeld, was Kurt Strametz. We met at KUZ so that I could have a look around and choose an open date. I told him what I was going to do, and he was excited because it was something different, something new.

While we were talking, he mentioned that he is a public speaking coach and that he had studied with Elfriede Ott. I was immediately fired up because I really admired Elfriede Ott. Unfortunately, she passed away on July 12, 2019, a great loss for the Austrian world of acting.

Since I was interested in working on my stage performance, not just my voice, Kurt Strametz came in handy. I had my first lesson with him shortly after our initial meeting. What I learned there in addition to my voice training was amazing.

How to move on stage, how to enter the stage and what type of gestures to make. I learned a lot of small details that ended up having a huge impact on my performance, for example: how to correctly hold the microphone.

I know, that might sound trivial, but watch people who have had practice and compare them to those who think they "know how to hold a mic anyway." ☺

I picked up a lot of tips that when applied together, resulted in a great performance overall. I spent many hours learning about how I came across on stage.

Listen to anyone speaking in front of an audience. There's a 90% change that they'll fumble over their words within the first minute.

Kurt, or Mr. Strametz, as I called him back then, had me do exercises that really made me break a sweat. It was really challenging, both for mind and body. Delivering a professional performance on stage is really hard work.

It was exactly what I needed at exactly the right time.

And that's what happens when you decide to do something; suddenly, you meet the right people at the right time.

And Kurt was (or is) like so many of the other people I met along my journey: supportive and helpful. Without Kurt Strametz, my life would have been very different. So, a big thanks to you, Kurt.

My first speaking event in March 2017 was, to say the least, not too shabby. Did I have an audience? Sure I did! Relatives, friends and acquaintances. Were there any other people there whom I didn't know? No clue. ☺

That evening I also learned a lesson about working with wireless microphones: take back-up batteries to every performance! ☺ Oh well, we learn from our mistakes, and that was definitely not the last time I learned a lesson while performing.

March 2017 kicked off a small tour of sorts, where I traveled around with my motivational program "RIGHT NOW!". A ticket cost € 24. I couldn't believe it; that was too expensive for a lot of people. They wouldn't even invest € 24 in themselves. Seriously? I was baffled. I had spent thousands on my own further development, working on myself so that I could help others, and € 24 was too much...

At some point it made sense. It might sound harsh, and it was a hard pill for me to swallow, but people knew that if they came to hear me speak, they'd actually have to do something with it afterwards. It's not a cabaret where you can sit back and be entertained. Although I have to admit, there were actually some people who came who thought it was a cabaret... which tells you a lot about my marketing skills. 😊

If you came to hear me speak, well, afterwards, you just might have to reflect on your life or even worse, work on yourself or make a change! I was disappointed! Bitterly.

I was renting location after location, doing performance after performance, and was watching my bank account dwindle down to nothing. I lost money at every performance. But the few people who did come to see me were thrilled. They were the type of people who were ready to act. People who approached me after the show, told me about their problems and asked for my advice.

After a while, I began to feel misguided. There had been this *voice* that propelled me to quit my job, so this must be the right path. Incidentally, I've never once regretted quitting my job. To this day, I can't imagine ever going back there.

But what was broken about this dream that had been *planted* in me? Why wasn't this getting off the ground? I decided to speak to the *universe*. "Hey, up there. I never would have had the stupid idea on my own to start my own business. That was your idea. So what's up? The voice was *very* clear. Thanks for that, and now it would be really nice if you could give me a sign about what to do."

I was pissed. I didn't believe in God. I had left the Catholic Church a long time ago. But I believed and still believe that there is *something* out there, something bigger than us. Now I don't just believe it, I know it. The last few years have been the proof.

Before I go more into my freelance career and my desperation, let's talk about the Catholic Church. This topic has been following me for years. I left the church, went back, left it again. I really thought about how it all works and whether or not there really is a God.

My conviction today is quite clear: yes, there *is* a God, but definitely not in the sense of the Roman Catholic Church. That also explains why it was hard for me to handle the word "God" for around 20 years. Whenever someone said "God," I went on the defensive. There is a book entitled: *Conversations with God*. It has crossed my path several times in my life, but I didn't want to and couldn't bring myself to read it because that one little word was in the title: "God."

Over time I learned to replace that word with another one and to interpret it in a completely different way. I said Universe, Life, Force, Shakti, or whatever word I could pull out of the different philosophies I was studying. In all of these cases it was a form of *energy* that was larger than us, which we can influence with our thoughts. And this energy of course never says anything else besides, "Of course, Sonja. Your wish is my command, Sonja." It never said that I couldn't do something or HAD to do something.

This energy was so different than the Catholic God. A man with a white beard who is constantly making rules where men can become priests, but women cannot. As a young girl in the Catholic youth group, that upset me a lot, because I wanted to become a priest but I wasn't allowed. That offended me, and I wondered why I was less worthy than a man in God's eyes. I was flat-out pissed. There were so many things that the church expected of me or told me I couldn't do just because I'm a woman.

After getting divorced when I was 29—although I had already left the church—I was no longer allowed to go to communion because I was divorced. So this God shuts people out who no longer fit his mold. You can't change your mind, and you can't make mistakes. You can only go to work like a good boy or girl, but if you make too much money, that's not OK either.

I joined the church again when one of my best friends asked me to be her child's godmother. I went to the priest in our town and was completely honest with him. I said I want to re-join the church because my friend is important to me and so is her child, and because I want to make them happy, but certainly not because I want to be part of the church again.

What happened next was a big surprise. The priest was just as honest with me as I was with him, told me that there was a lot about the church that bothered him, but that he wanted to help young people, give them a home and guide them through difficult times and that that is why he does what he does. We had a wonderful, open conversation. What surprised me a little back then was that I could still recite all of the prayers that I had to recite during the ceremony. I still knew them all. I didn't have to look at the text.

As children we are fed these prayers and we sing them in the choir hymns, but no one gives any thought to what they say, what they actually mean, what we are saying about ourselves.

Why don't we recite things like: "I am strong and self-confident"; "I can do anything I put my mind to, with diligent practice"; "I am worthy of being loved and I love myself"? We should learn to recite things like that early on and to internalize them – that is so much more important than looking to something bigger, some omnipotent power, while we are nothing but meek sinners.

And there's the code word "sinner", the word to cue my latest departure from the church. It was the day that my second husband's mother was buried. We sat in the church listening to a mass. I don't remember exactly how many times the words "sinner," "sinful," "sin," etc. came up; I think I stopped counting at 50. When we walked out of church, I felt small, *very* small. That guy up there (sorry, but that's all the respect I can muster), managed to make us so small and God so big in those 1.5 hours that we ended up leaving with a rock-bottom sense of self-worth.

That's not OK! I refuse to accept that! Now I understand why so many people go to church looking for help instead of taking their lives into their own hands. They believe that God Almighty has to fix all their problems because they themselves are worthless anyway! That's so far off! We all have enormous value and I will devote every single day of my life to showing and saying to as many people as I can: "YOU HAVE ENORMOUS VALUE. YOU ARE WONDERFUL."

**"YOU HAVE ENORMOUS VALUE.
YOU ARE WONDERFUL."**

I left the church again the day after the funeral and never went back. I made a decision! For good!

Then I received a letter that was obviously meant to scare me, where I was told that the Archbishop of Eisenstadt would be contacting me personally within the next few weeks for a chat. What was the point of that letter? By the way, I'm still waiting to hear from him. 😊

No, the church was and really is not my thing. But what about this God guy?

A friend of mine drew my attention to a book she was reading in 2019, *Conversations with God* by Neale Donald Walsch. I thought to myself: "Here we go again with that book." But I had learned to listen when *The Force,* or whatever you want to call it, would send me messages over and over again.

And so I bought the audio book and I couldn't put it down. I can really recommend Volume 1. Neale Donald Walsch was furious at the world and demanded answers from God. And God actually answered, spoke to him, and the result was this book.

It doesn't matter what you're thinking about the book at this point; I am the world's biggest skeptic and am constantly doubting stuff like this, but the God that I got to know in this book, he was a pretty cool guy. 😊 I liked him. That's right! That's how I imagine God to be. In this book, he also accounts for all the world religions. How cool! I was all the more astonished when I read when the book was written! 1994! It's now 2020! That was 26 years ago!

Why is this Catholic Church nonsense still being taught in our schools? Why are we still not showing our children the truth, who God really is and that we all carry a part of him or her inside of us? What I also like about this audio book is that God is female *and* male; sometimes a woman's voice is used, and sometimes it's a man's voice.

Since reading this book, I no longer get worked up when someone uses the word *God*. I personally still prefer words like *Life* or *The Force*.

But I digress. Back to my deep despair about the empty seats at my lectures. I followed every piece of advice from anyone I felt was qualified to give it. I didn't think about whether the advice was *good* or *not good* because these people were exactly where I wanted to be and so I did exactly what they did. They must know what they're doing.

One tip from me: if there are people out there who have exactly what you want, ask them for advice and do exactly what they tell you. Don't think about it. What happens when you overthink it? You start to question it. You start comparing the new information with everything you already know. And I'll tell you one thing in advance: these two bits of information will conflict. So what's the next logical step? You start to doubt. Of course! So don't think, just trust! And exactly *that* was the most difficult step in my development, until now. Learning to trust!

I'd like to explain trust using a metaphor. You enter a dark room and there's a light switch right by the door. Your goal is to light up the room. What do you do? You hit the light switch, and the lights come on. So you just trust that the light will come on when you hit the switch. But let's be honest. Do you really know how that happens? If you're not an electrician or a physicist, then probably not. Why does the light come on up on the ceiling when you hit a switch on the wall? That's right, a circuit is closed. And? What's next? OK, there's a flow of current! Right! But why? Why isn't it just *stagnant*? And what exactly is a current? If you know your way around a little, you already know that electricity has to do with negatively-charged electrons that migrate from the negative pole to the positive pole. And if you really know the ropes, you know that that's not true, because the technical direction of the current runs exactly in the other direction and it's actually about the electron opening that moves from the positive pole to the negative pole.

Confused yet? If you haven't studied physics like me, you most likely are. And that's good for our metaphor. Because who really cares how it works? Who cares whether electrons are flowing or stagnant and when they're flowing, from which pole to which. You just want the light to come on.

Your goal: to light up the room.
Step 1: hit the light switch.
Step 2: trust.
Step 3: enjoy the fruits - there is light.

With something as simple as turning on the light, you never think about HOW it happens. So why do you do that with everything else? Why do you always have to know exactly how things work in order to achieve your goal?

**We think too much
and trust too little!**

Now oftentimes, people make the mistake—especially if you are interested in energy work—of believing that if you just visualize something, it will come true. I just have to imagine the lights coming on, and they come on. In my opinion, that's not how it works. I believe that you do have to do something, but you don't have to understand exactly how it works. But in that aspect, I'm still very open to learning. If I'm ever able to turn on the light just with my thoughts, you'll hear about it in a new book. ☺

All day long, we trust in things that we don't understand. Or do you know how exactly the picture gets inside the TV? Do you know how to use a satellite dish to capture data that can then be viewed on TV? Or do you know how a cell phone works? No, you don't. But you still use one.

Incidentally, these last examples are always about forces that cannot be seen. ☺ Until the age of 20, I constantly said the following thing: "I only believe in things I can see." Once you study physics, you have to radically change that idea. You can't see magnetism, but it exists, and any child will tell you that. We all love to play with magnets. Or have you ever actually seen X-rays? Doubt it. And thank God we can't see the cell phone's electric waves either. I won't get into the influence those waves have on us and our bodies; that's not up for discussion here. But what I am saying is that there is more to this world than meets the eye.

By the way, there are also fields like that around our heart and brain. We have even learned to measure them. Since the middle of the 20th century, there have been repeated attempts to measure human fields and lo and behold, science has made some major advancements today.

There are now a number of scientists studying the brain-heart connection. When the brain has the same vibration as the heart, we are in our so-called flow. If that is not the case, we are stressed. And if we are in a state of trust, these vibrations coincide. But if we are constantly and desperately trying to keep everything under control, then we are stressed. But when we have things under control in a state of calm and confidence, then we are in our flow.

And I like having control! Really! But it took me years to distinguish between the two kinds of control, and to be able to live them out.

So the two kinds of control are:

1. desperately trying to control everything with your thoughts, planning everything down to the minute, leaving no room for mishaps and expecting everything to run perfectly;
2. enjoying life by making decisions, and trusting them. That means you know your goals, you live your life with focus, enjoy it, leave room for mistakes and accept when things don't go perfectly. Yes, that too is control. Keeping control through focus and trust, just in a much more relaxed state.

In Chapter 5 we will go into more detail about control and how the ice bath can help you let go. But I still haven't explained how I escaped my desperation.

I had been working with my best friend since November 2016. She had been supporting me for a year and we had hoped to make enough money for both of us. But exactly the opposite was true. We didn't make a dime. She called me in December 2017 and said she couldn't do it anymore. She was moving on to do her own thing. There I was, all alone. Well, not quite, I had my husband who was always there for me. But professionally, I was on my own. How was I supposed to handle the work that two people had been doing? But most importantly, who was going to take care of the website, the newsletter, my Facebook posts? She did all of that. Weeping fits, despair, hopelessness, total breakdown.

I was on vacation in Key West when I got that call. One of my bucket list goals was to go to the beach where Diana Nyad emerged from the water on September 2, 2013 after swimming the 110 miles (177 km) from Cuba to Key West. I first heard about Diana Nyad in November 2015. That's right, at Prof. Dr. Manfred Winterheller's Mind Management seminar.

Diana Nyad's story is long, but extremely important in this context. I'll give you the short version here to show you why it was important at this stage of my life.

Diana Nyad was born in 1949 and had a big dream as a young woman. Her dream was to swim the strait between Havana, Cuba and Key West, Florida. But before we get to her dream, let me tell you a bit about her life so that you know where it all began. Diana wanted to be a professional swimmer. She qualified for the 1968 Olympics in Mexico, but shortly before she set out on the trip, doctors diagnosed her with an infection of the heart. She was not allowed to swim at the Olympics and for safety reasons, she was also told not to swim short, strenuous legs. So no more 100 m or 200 m competitions for her. First you train hard for years and then you're not allowed to compete at the Olympics even though you have qualified; what a tough blow. Let's be honest, wouldn't WE have given up after that?

Not Diana Nyad. She switched to long distance swimming and set some records there, such as swimming around Manhattan in eight hours. And... she had that dream. She wanted to swim the strait between Cuba and Key West.

This *narrow* leg we are talking about is about 110 miles (177 km) wide, so I don't know why it's always called "narrow". 🙂

She attempted her dream in 1978 at the age of 28. She failed, then gave up her swimming career and her dream at the age of 30 and didn't put on a bathing cap for another 30 years.

By the way, she's not the only one who had attempted to swim the strait; since 1950, several long-distance swimmers have tried and none of them have made it.

In 2009, Diana Nyad turned 60 and the dream was still alive, a dream that she had failed to achieve 32 years earlier and now wanted to see through. People thought she was crazy, because she hadn't swum in decades and was in fact *already* 60. And I'm sure you know who I mean, those energy vampires who say: "At 60, you're too old to do that. You'll kill yourself."

Again, let's be honest, wouldn't we have thought the same thing? Wouldn't we have been one of those vampires? Before I dealt so much with this topic, I would have definitely been one. Now that I know what's possible with the right mindset and the right focus, I would react completely differently. I'd be supportive and encouraging.

Diana Nyad didn't let the naysayers stop her and she began training again at the age of 60. In the four years that followed, she made another four attempts and she failed once, twice, three times... but on September 2, 2013, on her fifth attempt, she managed to swim the 110 miles in just 53 hours. Her dream had become a reality.

She emerged from the water after crossing the strait. She was 64 years old and here's what she said:

I have three messages for you:

1. Never, ever give up.
2. You're never too old to chase your dreams.

3. It looks like a solitary sport, but it's a Team.

So what can we take from this story for ourselves? One of the most important things in life: "never, ever give up." If you have a dream, and it will most likely be something other than crossing the strait, then stick with it; don't give up. YES, you will fail; you will have setbacks, but it is important to keep going, and to not lose sight of your goal.

For that reason, it was so important that I was on that beach when I got that call and didn't know where to go from there. I was able to draw newfound strength there and I repeated Diana's words over and over again. "Never, ever give up. Never, ever give up."

Here is a photo from that important moment in my life. I am on the beach where Diana Nyad emerged from the water. The plaque honors her amazing achievement.

Photo: Josef Flandorfer

I'd like to share a word that I learned from Manfred Winterheller: synchronicity.

Synchronicities are "coincidences," in the sense of *happenstance* or *serendipity*. Something comes along exactly when you need it, when it fits perfectly into your life. Have you ever had the urge to call someone, and they call you right at that moment? Or do you look at the clock at the same time every day? For me, it's always 12:08 p.m. The funny thing is, that's my birthday. How can that be? Are there really such extreme coincidences?

I was always very skeptical about that, but now I not only believe, I know for sure that it's *Life, The Force, The*

Universe or whoever is out there speaking to us. *The Force* gives us signs. Sound crazy? Really? Did you read my last book? Among other things, self-experiments play a huge role.

You don't have to believe me. I wouldn't have believed it 15 years ago either. Good for you for continuing to read when I make claims like that... I think the old me would have put the book down. 😊 That means you are a lot further along than I was then. But if you still have doubts about synchronicity, I suggest you take a hard look at it.

I am constantly writing and saying something that will also appear a lot in this book: don't take my word for it; try it out.

Apply this to synchronicities; do little self-experiments. For example, look at the clock right now. Is it a *nice* number, like 10:10 or 11:11? Pay attention to the little coincidences that occur over the next few days. 😊

Here's an example of a synchronicity:

My daughter's boyfriend wanted to play in Dominic Thiem's first tennis tournament for amateur athletes (Thiem, Set, Match). Registration was closed, the spots were all taken and he didn't even have an ITN (amateur player's rating), which was a prerequisite for participation. But he wanted to take part with all of his heart. And so he made a decision:

Commitment! Trust!

And what happened next was incredible. The tournament was on Saturday. He wrote an email to the official address on Thursday evening. In the evening... after 8 p.m.!

He got an answer that same night. Someone had just pulled out, and there was one spot left. All he needed to do was name his club and provide his ITN number. Well, he didn't have either.

He wrote back and asked the very nice man by email whether he could add him to the ITN list. Two emails followed with various details, such as how to clarify his level of play, and on Friday at 6 a.m. it was clear: he would take part in the tournament on Saturday and be included on the ITN list.

So what can we take from this story for ourselves?

DO SOMETHING! MAKE A MOVE! Take the first step! Make a decision, devote yourself to it and trust!

Just because all the spots are gone and registration is closed doesn't mean there's no more chance. Would you have tried to get in under those circumstances? We give up way too fast. We think things are *impossible* just because it seems so on the surface.

If you really want something with all of your heart, and I mean it's a really deep wish, then absolutely anything is possible. I firmly believe in that and the last example is the proof.

What do YOU want with all your heart? Make up your mind, take the first step, and trust, and then watch carefully what happens.

**Over the next few days,
observe the *coincidences*.**

Back to what happened in Key West. I got the phone call where I heard that from now on, I was going to have to do everything by myself. The next day I stood in front of that plaque honoring Diana Nyad's success.

Is this really just a strange coincidence? I repeated the words, "never, ever give up", and was filled with hope. And the hope turned into joy. Finally! Finally! Finally, I can write my newsletter the way I want. Finally, I no longer have to argue over every word. Finally, I can write Facebook and Instagram posts the way I want and no longer have to justify it all.

My friend and I used to talk about everything so much that we often talked things into the ground. It took so much energy. Suddenly, I felt a sense of freedom. Now

I have the freedom to do what I want in the way I want to do it. Joy and a renewed sense of energy followed. As soon as I got home, I hit the ground running. My friend taught me how to manage the website, how to tinker with and post sayings, how to advertise on Facebook, and much more.

Thank you, Emanuela, for a year of valuable collaboration, for teaching me your craft and for everything that we were able to learn and experience together during that time. Thank you for growing with me. 😊

I decided to cut back on my speaking appearances and to trust. I couldn't do it alone. I had appearances planned through June 2018 and I still managed to pull those off. I also launched my one-day seminar "THINK NOW!". It was an upgrade from my "RIGHT NOW!" lecture. Eight guests attended the first seminar, and I don't mean eight paying guests. I invited five people who had helped me along the way, and one of them was my husband.

And this time, the same phenomenon was true: the few people who came were thrilled, but again, I lost money. I felt good because I had really helped people, supported them and helped move them forward. That was exactly what I wanted to do. Help people in a real way. But I had to make a living...

I had attended a lot of seminars, including a few sales seminars. How to sell effectively. How to get customers. How to sell yourself. How to explain your job. Learn your elevator pitch! Always have a business card on hand! Talk about your job every chance you get.

To be honest, I actually did all of those things because I was learning from the pros. And they were (and are) super successful people, at least from the outside looking in. So they have to know how it's done. All I have to do is exactly what they've done. Dead wrong. But why? Because it just didn't feel right.

First, I thought it was just fear talking. Fear of having to move out of my comfort zone. But I was doing that, over and over again, and it never felt right. Then it hit me: cold calling! And that was the hardest thing I had ever done in my life. My final school exams were easier. ☺

I just didn't get it. I couldn't get it into my head. Why did *The Force* send me all these signs and then make it so damn hard for me? Something was off. And then I thought about Manfred Winterheller again. He didn't do any of this stuff I was learning to do. At some lecture or seminar, he said something like this: "I don't actively sell; my customers come to me." That sounded like a core belief to me. He just believes that customers will come to him and that he won't have to actively convince them to buy anything. I liked that.

So—here we go again—I started looking at my core beliefs and my mindset, and I introduced affirmations. And the most important ones were:

Commitment! Trust!

I'm sure you've been paying attention and won't miss the fact that I just wrote a few pages back that you should do what the pros tell you to do. And that that's how you become one yourself. And now I'm telling you that I took that approach, but it didn't work for me. Isn't that a contradiction?

Yes and no. Check out what the experts are doing, try it out for yourself, and hold on to it for a while, but if it still doesn't feel right after a good period of time, then it's not right for you! Ditch it and find another role model. Someone who does things differently. Just like I found Manfred Winterheller for myself. No matter which expert I listened to, no matter which high-performance coach I learned from, I always got something out of it, but in the end, I consistently came back to Manfred Winterheller.

Sure, I picked up a few pointers from the others. In terms of positioning, I followed Bodo Schäfer very closely. I learned a lot from him, and got to know some other wonderful people who went on to shape my life.

Susanne and Axel were two of those wonderful people, ones who just *popped up* along the way. 😊

It is important to listen to a wide variety of coaches so that you have a choice, so that in the end, you can find *what fits* or gather the best of everyone and blaze your own trail.

But let's go back to June 2018 when I was working alone on my business, but had nothing lined up. My last speaking engagement was over.

I let everything go. Summer was just around the corner and I simply wanted to enjoy myself. No more pressure, no more selling, no more speaking engagements... I just wanted to let go, enjoy and trust.

In the meantime, I had developed a great deal of routines that helped me grow. I read tons of books, but of course, reading alone won't get you anywhere. You also have to implement what you read in the books.

Changing my core beliefs was a success. I received a request for September. The customers were coming to me. But during this speaking engagement, I realized what Bodo Schäfer meant when he said "I don't let companies book me for their employees. I only want to work with customers who come to me on their own accord." Companies often mean well when they book speakers. Some of the employees are grateful for the opportunity, but some are not at all. They just come because they have to, and they really drain the energy from the room.

That's exactly what happened in September 2018. Some of the participants were really enthusiastic and cooperative, but with others you could really tell how reluctant they were. At 4 p.m. sharp, one of the ladies jumped up and left. After all, the workday was over at 4 p.m. I carried on without letting anyone notice what I thought. I was professional enough by now to do that (something I had learned during my public speaking and stage training). But at the time, I wasn't enough of an expert yet to keep cool inside. I was boiling. How disrespectful and unappreciative can you be?

I talked to the organizer about it, who told me that unfortunately, that's always a problem. They try to offer something nice to the employees but they can't always reach everyone.

Exactly! I had already learned that. You can't please everyone.

You can't please everyone.

I had learned that, and I knew it in my mind, but it was still really hard for me to accept on an emotional level.

I couldn't let the disrespect reside where it belonged, with that person.

Incidentally, I realize that not EVERYONE will like what I write or what I have to say when I speak, but in my opinion, it is disrespectful to leave at 4 p.m. on the dot, although you know there are only ten minutes left. The company makes an effort, the speaker is working hard, and the guest shows no regard.

Today I know that for people who do things like that, it's nothing out of the ordinary. They're not happy, nor are they willing to invest anything in their happiness. You could say they are oblivious to good advice. 😊 Today I know that it's OK for certain people to live like that. Because we are all responsible for our own lives.

You too, are responsible for your own life.

YOU are responsible for YOUR OWN life.

For now, the story ends here in the summer of 2018. In the next chapter, I'll be telling you about qualifying to become a Wim Hof instructor. You'll clearly see how the first leg of the journey ("RIGHT NOW!" speaking engagements) draws to a close, and how the second leg (Wim Hof) begins to take off. And that's why trust is so important. It is important to let go to free yourself up for something else. But letting go doesn't mean giving up your dream or your goal, it just means no longer pursuing things that didn't work, but moving on to see what the next chapter of your life has in store.

Don't get me wrong. I'm not telling you that you can be a couch potato and pick your nose. It's about pausing for a moment, taking a breather and evaluating what options are still there. And I promise you, if you do that, you will always find an open door that you have yet to discover. ☺

4. My Training to Become a Wim Hof Instructor

I am writing this chapter particularly for those who want to know how I became an instructor and what the training was like. I get asked about it all the time. I have to say that the training course has changed a lot since 2018 and it's a very different today.

After completing Wim Hof's video course in 2017 and going for a swim in Neufeld Lake on January 1, 2018 at 10 a.m., I knew I wanted more. What else could I do? There was the training to become an instructor, more specifically, to become a Wim Hof instructor. I booked the advanced course for June 2018. I wanted to take it first before deciding whether I would also do the master's course and complete the full training.

The advanced course was a weekend course in the Netherlands, in Stroe, where Wim Hof lives. That weekend changed my life. Once again, a seminar helped me uncover a lot of what had been hidden until then. I think I could write an entire book just about that amazing weekend. 😊 But I will share just a few things that, for me, were extremely important take-aways.

First, an experience from a breathing session. Wim taught powerbreathing (a form of Wim Hof breathing). There were about a hundred of us, scattered across the room, lying on mats. This breathing exercise is extremely intense and only for advanced students. Among other things, deep-seated emotions come to the surface.

Of course, I was aware of that at the time, but I couldn't imagine it happening at all. I was a control freak, so what could possibly come to the surface? ☺ After a few rounds, I can't remember exactly when it was—and by the way, it doesn't matter—I realized how badly I needed to cry. I felt like I was going to burst, and I started tuning in to those around me. Nothing. Nobody was crying.

This voice in my head started saying: "Yeah, of course, you're one of the only women in here, and if you start crying now, you'll just reinforce the stereotype that women are crybabies." Then another voice came: "Sonja, you are strong. Don't you dare start balling. You're fine. You'll seem ungrateful if you cry now. What good will it do? And most importantly, *why* do you feel like crying?" That was a good question, a really good one. There was absolutely no reason, from a purely logical point of view.

There were nothing but great people there. People with vision, similar goals, and a great energy. So why cry? No idea!

A guy from Germany was lying a few feet away from me and suddenly starting crying, very loudly. I was so happy. It was such a relief for me not to be the first one to cry, as a woman. I couldn't hold my tears back anymore and so I started crying too, and then it was like a domino effect. Probably half of the participants were weeping or had tears in their eyes. So what was going on?

All I know is that something was released back then, even if I couldn't put it into words and still can't, but it just felt good and I have never felt that again. This feeling that something is stuck so deeply within me, and I can't let it out. I've also managed to let go of the belief that as a woman, I shouldn't cry because it would make me look weak. If I feel like crying, I cry. Period. End of story. And if I don't feel like crying, I don't. And I don't think to myself: "she's so cold; she doesn't even cry," which sometimes seems to be the case to the outside world.

So what happened inside of me? I learned to see things differently. I learned the lesson once again that we are all responsible for our own lives. I have learned, understood and felt that lesson so often, but that's exactly what is growing stronger and more intense inside of me.

I have TRULY understood what it means to take responsibility for myself. And I'll probably write that the same sentence again ten years from now, because life is an ongoing classroom.

Wim also delivered very inspiring speeches that weekend. One thing he always says is: "feeling is understanding!"

Feeling is understanding.

I finally got it that weekend. I got it because I felt it. I was—and am—an overthinker, and that's OK too. But even if you're the analytical type, it's important to really understand and feel things. If that sounds like gibberish to you now, I totally understand. 😊 My goal as the book progresses is to help you understand that last sentence by *feeling* what it means.

When we sat around with Wim and listened to him talk, we could really see his vision in his eyes. We could feel his mission in every sentence. At that moment, I realized what the difference was between him and the *experts* with whom I had learned. With Wim, it all came from within. He lived and breathed 100% of what he preached. He is authentic. He is, who he is. He doesn't pretend.

He makes this claim that he won't die until the medical books have been rewritten. His mission is this: he wants to prove that with breathing, mindset and cold therapy, you can control your own body. You can control your hormonal system and in turn, your immune system, yourself. And that is exactly what he has set out to prove, or has already proven.

Studies are extremely important to Wim because he doesn't want the Wim Hof method to be portrayed as esoteric hocus-pocus. He wants everything he says to be scientifically examined. That is very important for our logical minds. It's often the case that until we have understood something with our logic, we cannot grasp it in our hearts, and we cannot feel it. Manfred Winterheller works the same way. He always uses studies first as a basis for the examples he gives. It is important to first let some information penetrate us through our logic. The studies help support his statements. But then it comes down to trust, to energy.

I have adopted this approach in my seminars because it's easier to bring people on board that way. You lead them from the head into the feeling or, in my case, into the ice bath. There, you get a pretty good idea of what "feeling is understanding" really means. But more on that in Chapter 5.

After my inspiring weekend in Stroe, I was determined to complete the master's course in Poland in December 2018. Although apparently, I wasn't *that* determined. I received the study materials, and they were all in English. Now I can speak English and muddle my way through a conversation. Speaking English on vacation is no problem, neither is small talk, but we were looking at a series of studies here. There were complicated terms in there, like vasoconstriction or vasodilation, and those were the easiest ones. 🙂

I tried reading the first few bits and couldn't understand a word. How was I ever supposed to finish this? I wondered if I really should do the master's course; after all, I still had until August (it was only June) to think about it. By then, we were supposed to let them know for sure whether we wanted to do the training. I was fooling around writing my first book on the EFEU method© [original title]. Among other things, the book is about having goals, setting your focus, making a decision and implementing it.

So I just had to read my own book. 🙂 Did I really want to become a Wim Hof instructor? Yes! Well then, time to stop messing around! Set a goal! Focus! Go! Or in other words:

Commitment! Trust!

And look at what happens when you make a decision and commit to it! The energy that I had previously invested in fooling around was suddenly redirected into my studies.

I also had a mentor in Austria. He had become a Wim Hof instructor two years before me and was available to answer my questions. And I had a lot of them, but always got the same answer: "Go out of your head, go into your heart."

I wasn't sure what to do. Was he serious? I had very specific questions and wanted very specific answers. Is it really that hard? Today I completely understand what he meant or what he meant to say back then, but in autumn 2018 it was still difficult for me because with a "master's course mentor", I expected to have someone who answered my questions. For example, I wanted to know how the exam is carried out. But I didn't hear a word. That would have made me feel so much better...

But that's exactly the point that you need to hear, dear reader, in exactly the same way. We always want peace of mind. But peace of mind, and knowing in advance how things will play out, only provides a false sense of certainty. I got a hard lesson in that during the master's course.

In November 2018, the time had come. I drove to Poland, to a place that nobody knows and that no one would ever find by chance. *Certainly* no one gets lost and ends up there. 😊 But it was beautiful. Everything left in its natural state. You know, Wim Hofish. 😊

I arrived way too early, because you know, I always need my buffer time. I announced my name and asked for my room key. And the first challenge awaited me. There were no room keys. The rooms didn't have locks.

My thoughts started swirling: "But what if someone steals my stuff? What do I do with my valuables? I don't want just anybody touching my things!" When I think back on it today, it makes me laugh. The fears I was dealing with were incredible. And look at how hard it was for me to trust. I mean we were out in the middle of nowhere in Poland, after all. And bam, another one of those prejudices I had learned in my culture. 😊

The next shock came right after that. There were two Level 3 instructors on site. You are only allowed to train other instructors if you are a Level 3 instructor. Their names were Douwe van den Berg and Daniel Kluken (very experienced instructors). I asked them about the schedule, when I should be where and what time the meals would be served. They looked at me like I was from another planet and simply said: "The program is no program." Excuse me? Please tell me that's a joke.

I figured they must not have understood me correctly because I was nervous and we weren't all native speakers, so I asked again, in very simple language, what the schedule for today and tomorrow looked like. They gave me no answer, at least not one that I understood. They told me to let go, to trust and to just go with the flow.

How was I supposed to go with the flow if I can't create the flow because I don't know what's going to happen? I was mad. Not only because we had previously received zero information about what we would be doing that week in Poland, but also because nobody here had any idea. My worst nightmare had come true... the well-timed, well-planned Sonja had signed up to spend a week here and at no time of the day would she have any idea what was going to happen next. Welcome to hell!

It was reassuring, however, that several of the other newcomers felt the same way. That evening, we had the first official meeting and Daniel started right out the gate by explaining that the next person to ask about a schedule or a plan would be taking their shoes off and standing barefoot, in shorts and a T-shirt, outside in the snow for ten minutes. Wow, what a lovable guy. But he went on to say that the reason for that was for us to learn to be in the here and now. So we're not always looking to the future in our minds, but can enjoy more of the NOW.

I heard his words and understood what they meant, but how was I supposed to enjoy the now if I didn't know what was going to happen after it? I felt insecure, but curious and excited at the same time. All of the other seminars and workshops that I had attended in my life up to then had followed a schedule or a plan or at least set times and I knew when I had to be where.

I started chatting with the other future instructors and was fascinated. They had come from all over the world. They were from Canada, the US, Australia, India, Romania, China, Finland, Iceland, France, Hungary and who knows from where else? It was a melting pot of cultures and everyone added a little spice of their own. The differences in our simple, everyday habits were intriguing.

And I've got a funny story about that. There was a sauna in the lodging house and at some point, we all decided to get in it. Wim was in there too. I marched in with my towel tied tightly around me and got the surprise of my life. They all had their bathing suits on. Of course I was stark naked. It would never have occurred to me to wear something in the sauna. I wrapped my towel tighter and sat down with it still on. Later on, as I was chatting with some of the others, I found out that it was commonplace and completely normal for people to sit in the sauna in their bathing suits. They got the surprise of *their* lives when I explained that in Austria, we sit naked in the sauna.

Once the initial shock was over and I realized how many other habits there are in this world, and that all habits were completely normal for those who had them, it became clear to me once again in my life that it was nothing more than my upbringing and my environment that had to do with what I considered to be *normal*. I always said it in my lectures and knew that it was true, but that night in Poland it became very clear that "feeling is understanding." It wasn't until December 2018 that I REALLY got it, because I had felt it. There was no right and no wrong, there was just the fact that "I'm used to doing it this way, but others are used to doing it that way."

Of course I won't be writing about what actually did happen during that week, but one scene is still very important to me, because it helped me understand what Douwe and Daniel meant when they said that we should be in the here and now.

One beautiful day, or I should say one *cold* day, we were told to meet at 8 a.m. in front of the entrance. Appropriate clothing for 28 degrees Fahrenheit (2°Celsius). So in this case, that meant a swimsuit, slippers and a towel. 😉

We each had three buddies so we formed groups of four. Each group lined up behind another. We were headed for a river that wasn't too far away. We did exercises by the water, and in the water, and then went back. On the way back to the lodging house, Douwe reminded me not to wrap up in my towel. Man, I was cold!

Oh right, you see; this was the master's training to become a Wim Hof instructor, so you don't get to be cold. OK, Sonja, focus, breathe. I made it back. I wasn't cold anymore.

We stood in front of the lodging house and were looking forward to breakfast, which, in our opinion, should have been ready as soon as we went inside. Yeah... right! *IF*

WE WERE GOING INSIDE! As we were standing there in front of the entrance, Daniel and Douwe looked at each other and said: "And now, round 2." What happened at that moment was incredible. I started shaking like never before in my life. Why? What happened?

It was quite simple really. Once again, I was off with my thoughts in the future. I had kept my focus, mastered my breath and controlled my experience of the temperature, all the way up to the entrance. But once we got there, my mind wandered off into the future, to breakfast. I was no longer in the here and now. If you're not in the here and now when you're out in the cold, you'll freeze. It's as simple as that. ☺

So I had one thing to do: find my way back to the here and now. OK, show time: master the breath, regain focus... but I couldn't do it. My buddies helped me, put me in the middle so it wasn't as cold, used some tricks we had learned and eventually, I managed to calm down again. We went for another walk and made our way back to the lodging house. This time I said to myself: "That won't happen to me again." And I kept my focus and didn't think about breakfast.

Suddenly, Daniel said: "Go in and let's have breakfast." Right then, my focus dropped, I went in and had the afterdrop of my life. My entire body was shaking as the tension eased off. I could hardly get the food into my mouth. ☺

The life lesson I learned that morning was incredible. I realized how often I live in the future, how often I miss the now because I'm completely off somewhere else in my mind. It's not like I've been perfect about living in the now since that day, but I can bring my attention to it, I can focus better, and I notice it more quickly when I drift off. But most of all, I can enjoy the NOW moments much better and much more intensively. 😊

My second afterdrop, which I managed to get under control, was on the hike up Mount Śnieżka. That was our final test on the second to last day of that week.

Hiking up the Śnieżka in 5 degrees Fahrenheit (minus 15°Celsius), in shorts. This mountain always has two faces: one moment the sun is shining and a minute later you'll have a snowstorm, then sun again, then icy wind. Here, too, I had countless Aha moments and was extremely proud of myself afterwards for making it.

At my workshops, I always show the photo of Wim and me that was taken on November 29, 2018 on Mount Śnieżka, at a cozy 5 degrees Fahrenheit (minus 15°Celsius).

After this short photo session with Wim, we tucked away in a hut to warm back up. But it was a little too warm, and so the cold blood flowed a bit too quickly from my extremities to the middle of my body, and there came the next afterdrop. But this time I had it all under control. Horse stance (a specific movement in the

Wim Hof method), breathing, focus. It took me about 15 minutes to completely calm down again, but this time I had everything under total control, with a lot of fun and more importantly, with trust. 😊

5. Control is Good – Trust is Better. The Cold is Your Best Teacher

I only really learned how to trust from Wim Hof, or more specifically, from the cold, or even more specifically, from the ice bath! I have now conducted so many cold therapy sessions that I have lost count. I've had the privilege of meeting so many different people and getting a direct glimpse into their souls in the ice bath, so much so that I can say with 100% confidence that the following statement by Wim Hof is true:

He says: "You can't tell a lie when you're in the ice bath. You are in the here and now." And that is the truth. When I lead someone into an ice bath and look into their eyes, I can see deep into their soul. I see fear, panic, calm, struggle, pride, relaxation, trust, hardship, sorrow, exhilaration, and more. The ice bath brings it all to the surface.

Sometimes I talk to people afterwards because I want to know if I can help them in any way, but often people know exactly what I've seen and come to me on their own. With others, I can tell that it makes absolutely no sense to seek out a conversation with them, and with a few, it isn't necessary at all because they are deeply relaxed. 😊

So what's the *right* way to get into an ice bath?

An ice bath is stressful; it's a reflection of how you react to stress.

I would like to give a few examples of how people react in an ice bath. Some situations I describe in general terms and for others, I use names. Of course, I asked these people beforehand if I could use them as an example. For me, they are beacons of light who can be great role models for you and many other people.

Cornelia Daniel is a wonderful example of how you can move from control to trust. Cornelia is the owner of dachgold.at and the initiator of Tausendundeindach.at. She has ambitious goals, is a tough businesswoman and has a powerful vision. She works with photovoltaic systems. She has given me permission to write here that she was/is a genuine overthinker who has learned and is still learning—step by step— how to trust.

I got to know Cornelia in 2019 when we were both invited to speak at 24hours Leadership. I was immediately intrigued by her energy and one thing was clear from the start: Cornelia doesn't just do a job, she lives and breathes photovoltaics; she *is* photovoltaics. Her presentation was enormously inspiring and her vision was brilliant. But it wasn't just her vision that inspired; I was fascinated by what she had already manifested. A role model for the self-employed.

My contribution to the 24hours conference was also a lecture, then a Wim Hof breathing session and in the evening, an ice bath with the participants. The speakers, including the moderator Peter Stark, all jumped in on the cold fun. It was Cornelia Daniel's turn. I led her into her first-ever ice bath, which was about 33 degrees Fahrenheit (minus 1°Celsius). She managed to get in, had it all under control, but fell into a state of shock. I could see how much control she had over herself. When she got out, I asked her—well OK, it was more of a statement: "You're an overthinker; am I right?" I only found out later during a conversation that she got angry in that moment. Angry with herself. She didn't want to be an overthinker! She joined the others again to do the horse stance, and started repeating a mantra to herself. She had the mantra in her mind and was humming it softly.

A little later I asked Cornelia: "Would you like to get in again?" Determined and devoted, she slipped back into the ice bath, leaned back, closed her eyes and then asked a question that I had never heard before: "Sonja, do you mind if I sing something?" I said: "Go ahead, if it feels good to you." And she began singing a song that was incredibly fascinating. By the way, Cornelia also had an amazing voice; the hidden talents of Ms. Photovoltaics! 😊

She began to sing: "I release control and surrender to the flow of love, that will heal me." That was the mantra she had been repeating during the horse stance. She repeated that line over and over again and what I observed in Cornelia was phenomenal. First, she used willpower to get into the ice bath. She realized she had to let go to stay in, so she let go and wow, did she ever let go... 😊

She sang the song, sank deeper and deeper into a relaxed state and I would say she lost track of time. If I hadn't spoken up after a few minutes and said: "Well done, but now please come out before you fall asleep in there," she would have certainly stayed in for a few more minutes. Her face was a window to her soul, showing how she moved from control to trust and into a state of total relaxation.

It was amazing. She truly lived out the words:

Commitment! Trust!

You might be wondering why I'm telling you this story, and why it is important to us all. The ice bath is symbolic of stress. The ice bath puts the body under stress, and the body reacts to the ice bath in the same way it reacts to stress in our lives. In exactly the same way!

If we can learn to move from control to relaxation in an ice bath, and to trust, we can implement that lesson better and more effectively in our lives. If you experience stress in your life, say, due to an external or an internal stress factor like your thinking, you can draw back on what you learned in the ice bath and implement the tools you used to relax there. And that's how you build it into your everyday life. I promise you, life will be a lot easier once you have understood and implemented that lesson.

Sure, in order to get into the ice bath in the first place, you have to make a firm decision to do so and you need the determination to stay in, because your first impulse will be to jump back out. When you slip into the ice bath, that's when it's time to turn on your imaginary light switch. You turn on the light switch with the goal of relaxing in the ice bath, and then you trust that it will happen just as you've imagined. Like turning on the lights. You don't get involved or tell the circuit and the electrons what to do. If you did that, it would take forever for the light to come on, if it came on at all. And that's what it's like in the ice bath. You can't relax in there if you are desperately trying to control the experience or if you need to know how exactly it is working. There is only one thing you can do: you have to trust!

Commitment! Trust!

**And that is the secret
to a happy life! I promise!**

Trust is one of those tricky things. Most people find it really difficult. And the more workshops I give, the more

I realize how most people are stuck in their heads. And when I write "most people", I mean it. Maybe I just attract exactly those types of people. The fact is, 95% of the time, I meet people who are always trying to solve things in their heads. That doesn't exclude me, nor those who believe they are already so far along or on the verge of *enlightenment* (whatever that means in concrete terms). 😊

I used to be an absolute overthinker, caught up in my head from top to bottom and left to right. I thought that was the right thing to do, and I couldn't understand how people could just act on an impulse without questioning what they were doing. For me, those were *dreamers*, unrealistic people who will never amount to anything. Yep, that's right, I was very judgmental, but as an overthinker, you always are. You judge people, you judge situations, you judge things, life, the lives of others and above all: you judge yourself too! You're constantly judging.

And because it's what we've always learned, we believe that cold water is cold. Let's take water with a temperature of 68 degrees Fahrenheit (20°Celsius) as an example. Is that cold or warm? If we're in the sauna and then get into a 68-degree pool, it will feel cold. But if we're outside in below-zero temperatures in the snow and then get into a 68-degree pool, it will feel warm. In other words, our starting position is always responsible for how we perceive or feel things.

**Your starting position is always responsible
for how you perceive things.**

The water example was a metaphor, of course, but on the other hand, it should be taken literally. And that takes us to the ice bath.

I have a lot of people who say the following when they come to see me: "I'll listen to the theory, and I'll try out the breathing, but I don't know yet if I'm going to get into the ice bath." I have learned to take this with a smile because I know that it's exactly these types of people who do the most growing at one of these workshops. Most of these people eventually make it into the ice bath. When they get out, they are overjoyed, full of self-confidence and grinning from ear to ear. Those are the moments when I think to myself: "That's exactly why I do what I do." These are moments of joy, indescribable moments, that these people are sharing with me. Anyone who has experienced this before knows exactly what I'm talking about. 😊

But how is it that most of the participants end up getting into the ice bath at the end of a workshop? So you have an idea of how many people I'm talking about here, I have already guided over 1,000 people into an ice bath or a cold lake, and only about nine people refused to take part (as of July 2020).

In other words, less than one percent of the participants don't get in the ice bath after all. And it's important to say: that's OK too. Nobody HAS to do it. It is always voluntary.

But what happens in those hours before the ice bath? Why do so many people climb in despite their initial skepticism? It has to do with the message in this book. It has to do with your thinking and your attitude and getting out of your head and into a place of feeling and trust.

Both in theory and during the breathing exercises, the participants recognize and feel the importance of letting go – letting go of their thoughts, their doubts and their fear. And that's a very important topic with which a lot of people struggle: letting go!

I used to be a master at holding on to things and not being able to let go. That's why I understand my participants so well. But understanding it also means that I no longer accept it. I know what was possible for me and if I was able to go from holding on (and we're talking death grip here) 😊 to letting go, then anyone can do it. I am absolutely convinced of that. If I've managed to transition from being a frigophobic into an ice swimmer, then anyone can at least get into an ice bath. I am completely convinced of that too.

However, I learned one thing from giving these workshops. People have to come on their own accord. I've tried again and again to invite friends and to show them the benefits of the ice bath, but it doesn't work. If they come just to make me happy, but aren't driven by their own impulses, then they might get in because they trust me, but they jump right back out because they don't have the personal push to do it; they're just doing it for me. That's why at some point, I stopped inviting friends, because now I know one thing for sure:

It takes commitment to endure the ice bath. And to endure it with ease, in other words, to really enjoy yourself, you have to trust, trust in yourself.

Commitment! Trust!

By the way, it also works with commitment and control. You can withstand the ice bath too if you've made up your mind to get in, play it *cool* and tough it out. Those are often the people who have learned to endure unpleasant things or situations, to push through. These people can tough it out for a few minutes in the ice bath, but they've completely missed the point. Because the most essential step is skipped: moving into relaxation and trust. These people do it with willpower, with pressure, and with thoughts like "I can do this. I *have* to do this." It's really bad when you have friends at a workshop who feel like they have to outperform each other. Competition ensues and the ego takes over. When hiking in the cold in shorts, Wim Hof always says: "No Ego, We Go."

That's right; the ego plays a big role in many people's lives and I can recognize it immediately in the ice bath. In my workshops, I don't allow competitions and my leadership approach ensures that no one turns it into a competition. If someone seems to need an ego boost, I consciously push them to their limits so that they can learn that the ego and the ice bath don't go hand in hand. Everyone who has been through this with me was very grateful for the experience, because there are obviously not many people in their lives who would be willing to show them so clearly the limitations of their ego.

Mmmh... but I should clear something up, since I'm writing about limitations. I don't like limitations, and I'm convinced that we can do a lot more than we believe. But in my opinion, limitations should be expanded step by step and not with the help of the ego, but with trust. In other words, they shouldn't be crushed with brute force. We get rolled over enough in our lives, especially in those times when we learn through pain. As I talked about in my first book, there are two ways to learn. Through joy or through pain. But learning through pain is absolutely unnecessary if we can learn, step by step, through joy. 😊

So, back to our limitations. We can always be working to expand them, making small and sometimes huge leaps. But there is no point in approaching this with the ego, because it only puts us in danger.

Cold therapy is a great example of this.

The cold is a very good teacher.

The cold shows us our limitations, helps us expand them and warns us against too much ego, showing us when we are really relying on trust. You can't imagine a better teacher. The cold teaches us to find ourselves. The cold teaches us to relax. The cold teaches us to feel at ease in stressful situations. The cold teaches us to control our body through trust. Through trust, not tenacity and willpower.

Yes, I went from hating the cold—and I mean *really* hating it—to loving it. Now I love the cold, and am immensely grateful that the two WHs came into my life. *Winterheller* and *Wim Hof*, two beacons of light in my life.

6. Breathe Yourself to Freedom

One component of the Wim Hof method is breathing. When I say I'm a breathing coach, you wouldn't believe how often I hear people say: "Breathing comes naturally. I don't need a coach for that." Wrong! 😊

When you take a closer look at the breath, you suddenly realize so much about how your body works. What functions does the body actually perform and can we control them? Let's take a little journey into human biology.

Our autonomic nervous system consists of the sympathetic and the parasympathetic nervous system. Both systems are extremely important in our body. Since there are currently a great deal of books, studies and blog articles written about the autonomic nervous system, I won't go into detail here, but will give you a brief summary of the sympathetic and parasympathetic nervous systems. My goal is to demonstrate how many messages your body gives you and how you can learn to actively influence your body. And for everyone who is thinking: "Well, autonomous means that it works on its own and we can't exert any influence on it," I have a clear answer: I'm glad that it works on its own and that we don't have to consciously take every breath; otherwise we would forget to breathe every now and then. ☺. But it is possible to have an active influence on it and that's what this chapter is about.

And if you've taken anything from the book so far, you'll know that it's not just about having an active influence, but more about trust.

Let's start with the two main divisions of the autonomic nervous system.

The Sympathetic Nervous System

- Dilates the pupils
- Increases the heartbeat
- Inhibits stomach and intestinal activity
- Inhibits bile activity
- Promotes blood flow to the extremities

The Parasympathetic Nervous System

- Narrows the pupils
- Slows the heartbeat
- Promotes stomach and intestinal activity
- Activates the bile
- Promotes blood flow to the organs

The sympathetic nervous system is activated when we become active, when we are ready to perform.

The parasympathetic nervous system is activated when we relax, when we enter a state of rest.

Now a pop quiz for you: which of the two systems is more active nowadays? Right! The sympathetic! Our body is designed in such a way that these two divisions of the autonomic nervous system should be in balance. We should spend 50% of our time active and 50% in a state of rest. I deliberately write *should*, because almost nobody does. We forget to rest.

Some people think that they have to exercise to compensate for the stress they experience every day at work. It's a good idea in theory, but only if you are free from stress when you exercise. If exercise becomes an additional stress factor, it is counterproductive.

Let's look at a concrete example of this: a man works around ten hours a day in a highly stressful job, rushes to the gym after work, and does a full-power workout, which he hopes will help him really check out from the day. After three years, he drops dead. What happened? The stress in his free time along with the stress at work was a bad combination. The parasympathetic nervous system was never activated. Relaxation was completely absent and the body became overwhelmed. When the man dies, no one can believe it because after all, he exercised so much and exercise is supposed to be so healthy.

Yes, sport also creates a healthy balance, but not if it adds more stress to your life. We all think we're absolutely essential at work. I've heard that time and time again. I wrote about my burnout in my last book. I drastically cut back on my working hours, started training for a triathlon and lo and behold, I felt better very quickly. The point is not that I started training for the triathlon, but that I cut back on my working hours. And you know what? I still got my work done.

Over and over again, I see people performing at the same level even though they have cut their working hours. That's fascinating. In case you are someone who works too much, cut back on your working hours, and remember this:

Don't take my word for it; try it out.

People who want to lose weight, for example, often need nothing more than a little rest instead of the additional stress of a diet or some super modern form of nutrition. Look back two pages to the boxes about the nervous system. When is stomach and intestinal activity promoted? In other words, when does digestion begin? That's right, when you're relaxed! But if we never relax, how are we supposed to have a healthy digestion? It's obvious that the stomach and intestines do not work properly if we are under constant stress. When we stress ourselves out over food, we are actually achieving the opposite of what we want, just like with additional, stressful exercise.

But let's get back to breathing: breathing helps us balance our two systems. With the Wim Hof breathing, we go into a short state of stress and then back into relaxation. Incidentally, short-term stress is very healthy. It's only permanent stress that is unhealthy. If you want to relax, just breathe deeply into your stomach and slowly exhale again. Do that for just two minutes and you will already notice how relaxed you feel. You don't have two minutes to spare? Wrong! You just aren't taking two minutes for yourself.

It's easy to carve out two minutes. Cut it out of your social media time. ☺

By the way, social media is another stress factor. Oftentimes, we think we can use our breaks to surf around on Facebook, Instagram, Xing or some other platform. But that's not a real break, at least not for the brain.

Your brain is fed more and more information and just keeps on churning. Afterwards, it's much harder to concentrate and we get tired more easily. If you want to know more about that, I recommend the book *Deep Work* by Cal Newport. The book is about how to focus better. One important point here is to switch off or avoid social media.

One thing you can definitely do is set aside two minutes to breathe. You will be doing your body an enormous amount of good. You don't believe me?

That's OK. You don't have to believe me, but at least try it out!

If you can carve out more than two minutes, then try the Wim Hof breathing technique. Download the Mini Class from the Wim Hof website and get started.

In this book, you won't find any instructions on Wim Hof breathing. But I can highly recommend visiting a Wim Hof instructor and learning the breathing technique.

It has so many positive effects, that your immune system will get an enormous boost. There's an increase in oxygen in your muscles and tissues, you become more alkaline and more endorphins are produced. You will feel really in touch with your body and mind.

How often do you get in touch with your body and go into deep thought?

Anyone who meditates knows exactly what I mean. The special Wim Hof breathing technique helps you reach a spiritual state that people who meditate for years often can't achieve. It takes a lot of practice to see various *lights and colors* during meditation. This can be achieved very quickly with Wim Hof breathing.

What's the point? I could list a few of the advantages here, but I won't; I'll leave it to you and your body. Again, Wim says: "feeling is understanding", and that's the truth. You will understand it once you do it and experience it, or in other words, once you feel it.

There are certain things in life that you have to feel in order to understand them, things that cannot be explained. How can you explain being in love? Words cannot express what you feel when you are in love. You can only feel it.

So try out some breathing and feel!

**Again, don't take my word for it,
try it out yourself.** 😊

6.1. Practical example

In November 2019, I offered a breathing and mind management workshop exclusively for advanced students of Dr. Joe Dispenza's work. An ice bath was not planned into the weekend.

The breathing session with this group, which had a lot of experience with meditation, was really quite deep. Christine Huber was one of the participants. She completely lost herself in the breathing, allowing herself to fall very deeply and after a while, she noticed that she could no longer move. Now don't worry, that's not to say that you would experience the same thing. 

Christine's body was reflecting the current state of her life. She was living in a metaphorical corset, which she had put on herself, and she couldn't move. She had already managed to let a lot of things go at a few of Dr. Joe Dispenza's retreats, but our breathing session showed her what was still missing.

After the breathing session, I had a private conversation with Christine. We talked about her *corset* and what it took to break out of it. I gave her my book about the EFEU method©, briefly explained what it was, and she recognized that she had some work to do. Work to break out of the victim role and take control of her life. Meditation is a good tool, a great one really, but there are certain things you just have to tackle in real life that you cannot meditate away. ☺

And nothing against Dr. Joe; on the contrary, I like him. I watch all of his videos and I think he's great. One of my favorite books of his is *You Are the Placebo*. I recommend it at all of my seminars. But what I notice again and again with his students (I work with them pretty often now) is that they get up at 4 a.m. and meditate for 90 minutes (I was one of these people), but that they don't incorporate that energy into their everyday life.

Dr. Joe Dispenza says that you should take the feeling of meditation with you into your day, but it's difficult for most people to maintain the feeling throughout the day. The breathing training can complement this beautifully. You can bring yourself back to the feeling of meditation with a few simple breaths, consciously taken throughout the day.

And the breathing session on that weekend with Christine showed the participants over and over where exactly they were in their lives. The same was true with Christine.

But that's not all! Christine was curious, and wanted to try out the cold. During lunch, we realized that many of the participants were curious about trying out cold therapy.

One important thing that you learn when you become a Wim Hof instructor is how to *live in the moment*, and I am now really good at that. So Jürgen (a friend who was helping me with the seminar) and I tossed our afternoon plans overboard and went for a dip in the cold with the participants. Luckily, there was a nice cold river nearby.

About three quarters of the group was curious and embraced the icy adventure with Jürgen and me, and by the way, this was in late November. And, of course, we hadn't planned a cold therapy session, so not everyone had a bathing suit, but they all had on undergarments, and that was good enough for a cold bath. 😊 That's what I loved about that group; they were spontaneous and up for an experiment. They lived according to the motto: "I've never done that. Let me try it out." 😊

Christine was there too, of course, and slipped into the cold river. She was able to let go of a lot in there; she enjoyed it and felt really happy. Let's stay with Christine for a while, but move on from the workshop. She went home at the end of the weekend and did two things:

1. She took control of her life and began doing and saying things that she would have never done or said before.
2. She went for a dip in her pond every day in winter and began to love the cold water.

We have a phone call once every couple of weeks and life as a whole has been much better for months. The breathing and the cold have had a positive effect on all areas of her life.

She now helps me with my workshops and in winter, she goes swimming in the lake with the participants. She also guides groups into cold rivers. She is becoming more and more in tune with the cold and with nature.

The most important thing she has learned is to silence the noise in her mind and find her focus again. Christine draws on this every day, making the conscious decision to follow her focus.

When I let Christine read this passage to see whether I had perceived everything correctly, she asked me to add the following: she realized that only she can break free from her corset from the inside out, and that's exactly what she did. Breathing provided a pillar of support along the way.

In our fast-paced world, we believe we have to solve every issue on the spot, but take your time and, above all, give yourself time.

Was Christine's corset gone overnight? Of course not. But it is loosening up more and more, little by little.

Maybe you don't believe that breathing and cold therapy can have such a tremendous impact? That's fine. Try it out. As you know:

"Feeling is understanding"… so *feel* it for yourself. 😊

7. Poland, Wim Hof Winter Travel, February 2020

Wim Hof Winter Travel in Poland. A unique experience. So what do they do there? How do they manage to do what they do?

In February 2020, I was an instructor at one of Wim's Winter Travels in Poland. I led a group of 20 young men along with another instructor named Tim. We stayed at Wim's house, and it was an unforgettable week for both the participants and the instructors. About 100 people took part in the winter expedition, including nine instructors. Wim Hof joined us for the breathing sessions with the participants, jumped with us in the cold water and of course, went hiking in his shorts with us on one of the days. Our group was called the *Cold Brothers & their Cold Mother*. 😊 That's right, I was the Cold Mother.

You can learn a lot from a week like this. I'll pick out a few points that I think are very important.

The first point is about the strength of the group. Peer pressure can be good or bad. But let's not judge that yet. Usually, we allow ourselves to be dragged along when several people are doing the same thing. We humans don't like to be outsiders; we prefer to swim with the current.

That's what happened in Poland, and it was a very positive thing, because each and every one of us was able to push our own boundaries, without completely violating them. The instructors make sure that's the case. Our boys took their first ice bath; the goal was to stay for five minutes in Wim's famous swimming pool behind his house. Famous because it appears in almost every documentary about him. 😊

Some of the Cold Brothers were scared or didn't think they could do it. Of course, it was up to us instructors to motivate them and boost their self-confidence so that they believed they could do it, but they had to do it themselves. And each and every one of them did it. Afterwards, we could read the pride right off of their faces. It was wonderful to see them beaming with pride and to observe the boost in self-confidence in those short five minutes. And all of them made it because of peer pressure, among other things.

Especially those who were afraid and didn't think they could do it were cheered on by the others. Not forced! Just motivated! There's a huge difference. Everyone had the opportunity to say no. And we instructors could see in each individual's eyes how they were really doing and what they were feeling. It took effort to overcome their fears, and afterwards, we saw pride and pure bliss.

We also got a lesson that week on how Wim really thinks. Sometimes it's difficult to understand his answers to your questions, and you need a lot of experience in mind management to know what he means. For him, certain things are completely logical, but for the *average person*, they're a mystery, things like trusting in your own body.

One evening, all of the participants were sitting with Wim asking questions, one after the other. Many of the questions were asked twice, because for a lot of people it is really tough to understand how Wim endures what he endures. I want to pick out a question that fits in well with this book.

One participant, a cardiologist, evaluated Wim Hof's studies in detail and concluded that they made a lot of sense. One of them was the famous Michigan study. For this study, Wim wore a suit with built-in tubes. First, cold water was pumped through the tubes, then warm water. An MRI was included in the experiment. Everything that could be measured in and on the body was measured from head to toe. Pictures were taken of his brain activity and, among other things, the internal temperature of the body was measured. One very interesting measuring point, however, was the surface temperature of the skin, and that's what I would like to talk about in more detail. But first, if you'd like to know more about the studies, go to the Wim Hof website at www.wimhofmethod.com and check out *The Science* under *The Method*. There, you can read about all of the studies, and current ones are always being added.

But back to the Michigan study. A control group also wore this particular suit and the surface temperature of their skin was measured. The completely logical result was: when warm water was pumped through the suit, the skin was warm and when cold water was pumped through, the surface temperature of the body dropped. This generated a nice curve on the graph, spiking and falling. It was the same when Wim Hof was evaluated; he generated exactly the same result. So far so good.

But the next day, he was told to do what he always does (his breathing exercises), and then the experiment was repeated. He performed his breathing technique and then—as he told the cardiologist—he turned his attention inward and simply trusted.

Commitment! Trust!

The result: he was able to maintain the surface temperature of his body at a constant level. Let me repeat that: first, cold water ran through the suit, then warm water, and he managed to keep the temperature of his skin constant.

The cardiologist in Poland was obviously not quite satisfied with Wim's answer, and asked: "Yeah, but HOW did you do it, Wim? Did you visualize fire? Did you put on a protective layer in your mind? Did you work with colors?" Wim said he trusted and left the rest up to his body. He didn't do anything. But trust!

I love that answer and I really understand it! Finally! After more than 15 years of mind management work, I can understand answers like that. I hope you're on a faster path than me and it won't take you 15 years to grasp what trusting in yourself and your own body can do. 😊

It's often not about what you do or think, but simply about having trust. Have you ever suddenly had an impulse to do something and you don't know why, but you just do it and it feels right? In an instant, your impulse leads to a good conversation, a new business deal or maybe you meet someone *by chance*, simply because you had the urge to turn right instead of left.

We don't trust nearly enough in those impulses; instead, we switch on our brain and think: "That's crazy. What good will that do? I'd better not." A lot of times, we even degrade ourselves by thinking: "Sometimes I have such stupid thoughts. What gave me the idea to turn left now? I have to turn right."

Wim Hof listens to these impulses a lot. I call it our inner voice. I don't really care whether you call this *voice* your gut feeling, intuition or inner voice, or whether you call it following your heart. 😊 It's just an impulse that comes from within and that we should learn to trust again.

That week in Poland with Wim Hof, the eight other instructors and the 100 participants, showed me again how much we are wrapped up in our heads and how important it is to believe in ourselves, and to recognize our abilities, especially in relation to our body. I started to understand the notion of *mind over body* even better. We are in charge of our bodies and can influence our immune system.

What? Has Sonja lost her mind? We can influence our immune system? Yes, we can! We can strengthen it and there are several ways to do this. The Wim Hof method is one of them. I won't bore you here with studies; instead, check out the Wim Hof website and the section on *The Science*, where you will find, for example, the Radboud University Medical Center study from 2014, in which Wim and 12 other test subjects prove exactly that: namely, that we can deliberately influence our immune system. You can also find some videos about this on Wim Hof's YouTube channel or check out www.keep-on-cooling.com.

Or conduct your own experiment, because like I say:

Don't take my word for it; try it out.

Take a cold shower every day and compare how often you get sick now to the past few years. That's it. 😊

8. Society, Prejudices and Morning Routines

This chapter is about getting to know what makes our society tick, why we are the way we are and what changes we can make with small steps.

These small steps are very often found in literature; there are countless books that talk about them. One of my favorite books is *Atomic Habits* by James Clear.

Manfred Winterheller also uses the small steps principle. His method is called SSR (Slicen, Slowen, Repeaten [Slice, Slow, Repeat]). I also wrote about that in my first book, drawing on inspiration from the book *The Slight Edge* by Jeff Olson, which teaches us to move forward with small but consistent steps. My method is called the TeLaWi (Teilen, Langsam, Wiederholen [Divide, Slow Down, Repeat]) method. If you're thinking: "Sonja totally copied that," take a look around at some of the successful speakers in the German-speaking world and then go to a Tony Robbins event. You'll realize that everyone copies from everyone. Is that a bad thing?

No! On the contrary! Everyone gives the content their own personal touch, which means we can all reach different types of people. And that's why it's a good thing! So more people can be reached. We aren't competitors; we actually all have the same goal in the end: to make this world a little better, and to make people happier. ☺

So it doesn't matter whether you call it SSR, Atomic Habits, The Slight Edge or TeLaWi. If you compare all the books and bits of wisdoms on this subject, the truth is that they all say the same thing: instead of taking on a huge task from one day to the next, take small steps. If you attempt to radically change your entire life overnight, you'll see that it's impossible to stay the course. You will inevitably fail. The most scientifically-based book I've read about this is *Atomic Habits*. It gives a clear explanation about how the brain works and the best way to change our habits. In a nutshell: TeLaWi.

If you continuously take small steps that are relatively easy to take, and that are quickly achieved, then you will persevere and end up changing your life for good.

The TeLaWi method is explained in detail in my previous book, but it makes sense to repeat some of it here.

So why should we take small steps? Why can't we just change our entire behavior in a single second with one firm decision?

Let's start from scratch. Humans are herd or pack animals, which means we want to belong. Being part of a group gives us recognition and respect, and makes us feel safe. In the past, separation from the tribe into which one was born was equated with a death sentence; surviving alone was hardly possible.

Today, this model of the human being belonging to a tribe is represented by the family. And this is exactly where we adopt our first habits. So how does this work in the brain? I'll just give you a simple, on-the-surface explanation. For more detailed information that dives deep into biology, I recommend books by Dr. Joe Dispenza or Dr. Bruce Lipton, and many others (again, refer to "Buchertipps" [Book Tips] on my website: www.keep-on-cooling.com).

For the book you are holding in your hands right now, and in order to implement the concept of "Commitment! Trust!" into your life, a quick introduction into how our brain works will be enough.

We observe other people's habits and store them in our brain as *normal*. Nerve pathways are linked together in our brain and the more often we see, do and experience certain things, the better and more quickly these nerve pathways connect. If we practice something long enough, it becomes automatic and a habit develops.

One simple example is learning to walk. When we are babies, we see people walking, and at some point, we try it out ourselves. After about 8,000 attempts, we can walk upright. It is the same with language. We will learn to speak based on what we have learned from our environment. So one thing is very clear: we don't choose our first habits ourselves. We are shaped by our environment.

Now, of course, there are also habits that are not so great, such as regular consumption (abuse) of alcohol, physical aggression, family arguments, chocolate as a consolation, and so on.

Many people then use these experiences as excuses when they grow up, and end up acting exactly like their parents. Then they say: "I can't help it. I was brought up that way." Well, I won't let you off the hook that easily. 

Once we grow up, we can make our own decisions. YES, I have to admit, breaking old habits is not always easy, but it is definitely possible. Everyone can do it, and people do it all the time. There's one pre-condition though: you have to want it! And that takes us back to:

Commitment! Trust!

And please don't say: "OK, I'll give it a try." or "Well, it's worth a try." A try? Where is the commitment, the determination? It took you 8,000 attempts to be able to walk, but you expect to change a habit with one try? In all honesty, we often make things far too easy on ourselves and slip comfortably into the role of the victim.

But enough with the morality lesson; let's go back to how we can change our habits using the TeLaWi method.

Who else do we adopt habits from? From people who are constantly around us, so from the masses (society), our culture and from our role models. By role models, I mean people who have a certain charisma, who are powerful (although power unfortunately has a negative connotation in our society, but when I say power here, I mean it in a completely neutral way. I believe that power can be very positive if it is used in the right way, to help people).

Since the people with whom we spend the most time shape us the most, it is important to take a closer look at your surroundings. Do you want to be just like the people around you? What is the culture like in the country where you live? Do you like it?

As described in Chapter 4, I was exposed to so many different cultures during the Wim Hof master's course that I can say today that we Austrians are quite unique. 😊 Especially when you take a look at some of the smaller communities in Austria, there are habits there that seem completely foreign to me. One of them, for example, is gossiping about people who don't fit perfectly into the community's mold, like people who have moved into the community or were raised in the city. In Austria, we generally condemn anything that we don't understand or know.

In the master's course, I got to know so many open-minded, non-judgmental people. As you can see, there are other ways to live than the way we live in Austria.

Or let's look at something simple: people's eating habits. The *omnivores* attack the vegans, the vegans condemn the meat eaters and the vegetarians are lost somewhere in the middle. Then there are the Keto fans who demonize carbs and those who vilify lactose, because lactose is *really bad* for us. And everyone thinks that THEIR path is the right one.

Why can't we all just accept each other for who we are? Because we always believe that the way WE are is the right way, the way WE think is the right way to think, and the way OUR culture prescribes things is the right way to live. Why do we think that? Because we're so used to it and anything we're used to feels right, at least until we see something else that we like better. 😊

Personally, I prefer to be the way I want to be. Of course, that means that I have to let others be the way they want to be. That's called acceptance, a value rarely found in our culture, but one that I have adopted in my life. Freedom of expression and acceptance.

How about you?

Can you let others be who they are? I used to have a major problem with that. It was a learning process, and that's the perfect lead-in to our next topic: change!

My *favorite phrase* is: "We can't change that; we've always done it that way!" I'm sure you can imagine that when I say that's my *favorite phrase*, I'm being sarcastic. As soon as you blaze your own trail and make changes, you no longer fit into the mold or the environment from which you come. But change is so extremely important. I'm sure you've heard the famous quote from the Greek philosopher Heraclitus:

**"The only constant
in life is change."**

Everything changes on a constant basis. But when you make changes that don't coincide with your environment, you will be met with judgment and condemnation.

So how do we still find the courage to change, to break away from the norms that don't suit us? We just look for a group of people who tick the same way. We look for role models who live the way we want to live. Think about the type of person you want to be, the type of life you want to lead.

Don't think first about whether or not it's possible. I can tell you one thing from the start: it *is* possible. But we often can't see it at the beginning because we are too busy thinking about HOW it will work. The *how* always gets in our way, so there's only one thing to do:

Commitment! Trust!

Make a decision to be the person you want to be and trust that life will line up. Does that mean you can plop down in front of the TV and just trust, and everything will take care of itself? Some people believe that, but I don't. I think you have to actually do something, and from a purely biological point of view, that makes sense.

Think about those nerve pathways in your brain. If you want to create new structures, you have to build them. So how do you build them? Through TeLaWi, so by practicing and repeating, just like when you learned to walk or speak.

For over 15 years, I have tried a lot of different things with the goal of changing my life in a way that leaves me happy and content. And what do you know... the most suitable solution is presented in this book.

I toyed around with this for a very long time, in particular, with how I can be sure that I will pull it off, because at first, it was no different for me than for everyone else: two weeks fully motivated with a sudden drop in drive, and then I found myself falling back into my old patterns and habits.

8.1 Morning routines and all that jazz

Morning routines are all the craze right now, and there are a plethora of strange ideas and possibilities out there. The best thing to do is to get to know which morning routine works for you by simply trying out a few of them. Let me tell you about a routine that I stuck with for around five months, before ditching it because I was constantly exhausted.

I would get up at 4 a.m., head to my meditation room in the basement, and do one of Dr. Joe Dispenza's meditations. They last between 60 and 90 minutes. Then I would do a workout followed by some strength training, one last round of cardio or some stretching. Around 6 a.m., my husband would get up and we would practice Wim Hof breathing together. Then we treated ourselves to a nice cup of coffee and a casual chat.

The advantage back then was that I was totally tired in the evening, would fall into bed around 9:30 p.m. and sleep like a baby. The disadvantage was that, over time, I grew more and more exhausted throughout the day. I would lay down for a few minutes, but after that I was even more tired and completely unable to concentrate. At some point, I decided to stop getting up so early.

I had chosen that morning routine because 4 a.m. is supposed to be the best time to meditate. Today I can say: yes, that might be true, but not for me. ☺ Before starting that meditation routine, I had tried out about ten different other morning routines, but couldn't stick to any of them for more than a few months.

For the past year, my routine has looked like this: my husband and I get up together at 6.30 a.m., practice Wim Hof breathing, watch our mind movies, do three strength training exercises and then we have a cozy cup of coffee together.

It feels good and, above all, stress-free. I stopped putting so much pressure on myself to do everything my role models say. I believe that everyone has to find their own ritual. There is no morning ritual that will suit all of humanity and is the only right way to start the day.

But there is one thing that applies to everyone: hands off your cell phone in the morning. I am really serious about this one, and I'm speaking from experience. If you wait until later in the day to turn on your cell phone and, in particular, to check social media, you will have a much more energetic, relaxed and happier start to the day. The same goes for the radio; keep it off, and please don't listen to the news in the morning.

You don't think it matters that much? OK, let's test it out. Listen to the news, then turn off the radio and see how you feel. Really look inward at how you feel, and pay attention to your thoughts. What thoughts are running through your head?

The next day, don't listen to the news. Play your favorite music; listen to three songs you like and then turn off the radio. Now pay attention again to how you feel. What do you feel and what are you thinking about?

If you complete this self-experiment, you will see what I mean.

But don't take my word for it! Try it out!

Our morning routines shape our mood. You'll have a completely different start to the day if you only surround yourself with positive, pleasant things. That's a promise!

Now, you probably noticed that I said something about a mind movie. What is a mind movie? Let me explain it briefly here:

We have already talked about the nerve pathways in our brain and how they are established, namely when we deal with the same things over and over. And in the same way, the more often we hear a sentence, the more likely we are to believe it. As a child, if you constantly heard: "You're stupid," then you will believe that you are stupid. If you want to intercept these pathways in your brain and instead, choose to believe that you are smart, then keep telling yourself that you are smart, until you start to believe it.

Yes, that's right, these are called affirmations. There is a lot of argument about whether these work or not, but like I always say: give it a try and see for yourself. But please don't only try it twice, then say that it doesn't work and give up. TeLaWi, people. Repeat your affirmation once a day, every day for a few weeks or months and you will notice an obvious change.

So, back to these mind movies. As I said before, we learn through our external experiences, through words, images and music. Affirmations are just words, for example. But you can increase the intensity of these words a great deal; in other words, you can sort of turbocharge your affirmations by reinforcing them with pictures and music. You insert one picture after another into a video, place an affirmation over top and have music playing in the background. That is known as a mind movie, so it's your very own film that redirects the nerve pathways in your brain.

If you want to see what a health-based mind movie looks like, go to 888lifechanger.com and click on Mind Movies. You'll find some good examples there. I recommend, however, that you tinker around with making your own mind movie or have 888lifechanger make it for you if you (like me) don't want to or don't know how to edit videos.

If you watch your mind movie every day—and I do this once in the morning and once at night right before bed—you will be *reprogramming* yourself step by step. In other words, using small steps with a lot of repetition. You'll read the affirmations over and over, which then establishes new neural links in your brain. Instead of "I'm stupid" or "I'm not good enough and can't do it anyway," after a few months, you'll be certain of things like "I am smart," and "I am good enough and can do this!".

I'm sure you're wondering right now whether this really works. Is that all I have to do to change my life? Yes! I stand behind this 100%! Why? Because I've seen it firsthand. And anyone who knows me knows that I only pass on tips that I have tried out myself and found to be good. 😊

But let me ask one thing of you: be patient. The TeLaWi method isn't something that works overnight. You can't change a core belief that you've been hearing for 20 years in one single day. That's simply not possible. But then maybe that's just one of *my* core beliefs and you can in fact do it in one day. If so, please write me an email; I'd love to know how. 🙂

Actually, it does work in the short term, like anytime you go to a seminar, read a good book or complete a coaching session. You're full of motivation and you believe that anything is possible. But after two weeks at the most, you lose the faith because the people around you drive you back into your old habits. You surround yourself with the same people, have the same job, and the same problems as you did before the seminar. Your environment won't change if you don't change.

That is exactly why I wrote down everything I could at Dr. Prof. Manfred Winterheller's seminar in November 2015. Back home in my old environment, I transcribed everything into a beautiful book and read it every day. Back then, I hadn't heard about mind movies, but I had already recognized that I had to repeat the content over and over again if I wanted to stick with it and implement the things I had learned.

Is it a lot of work? You bet it is! I am always amazed at people who actually believe that everything around them will change, but that they don't have to change themselves. We are often simply too lazy to change because it takes work. And that's exactly where TeLaWi comes in. Te stands for *teilen*, or divide. Divide your change into steps that are so small that you will actually take them! Make sure it's easy and doesn't involve a lot of work.

Start with something simple like not turning on your cell phone in the morning. Go into the bathroom, look at yourself in the mirror and say to yourself: "You are a great person. I like you." If that goes well, then at some point you can switch to "I love you." You can keep changing it until it feels right.

8.2. Prejudices about cold therapy

Since this book is also very much about cold therapy, I will talk about society's prejudices using the example of the cold.

There are the all-time classics that many of us heard in childhood, such as:

a) "Put on some clothes. You'll catch a cold!"
b) "Don't go outside with wet hair. You'll catch a cold!"
c) "Don't go outside barefoot. You'll catch a cold!"

Those are just three examples of the classics we've all heard. So where do these core beliefs come from (because that's all they are, core beliefs)?

For that, we have to take a look at how we live today. We live in spaces that are heated in winter and cooled in summer. We live within an average temperature range of 68-73 degrees Fahrenheit (20-23°Celsius). When we leave our home in the winter, we put on nice, warm clothes, and are often packed up in several layers. I know all about that, by the way. ☺

So what does our body experience there? It no longer has to adapt to the challenge of being exposed to temperature fluctuations. And any skill that our body no longer needs, it forgets.

Look at a muscle that is no longer used, for example, because the leg is in a cast. The muscle mass diminishes, simply because it is no longer being used.

It's the same with every other function in the body. If we don't use it, we lose it. If we never expose ourselves to the cold, we will no longer be able to cope with it; by the way, the same goes for heat. Hence the phenomenon of the sudden heat waves in the summer. It's not that we are having heat waves, but that we can't stand the heat anymore because we have A/C in our living spaces and in our cars.

I admit that a car trip with A/C is a good thing; the only question is whether it is absolutely necessary at all times and everywhere.

What I definitely know is that when it's cold, it is *not* necessary to wear so many layers or to turn on the heat full blast. Our bodies can handle the cold very well. They are designed for it. How else do you think our ancestors survived?

Today, we're quite simply a bunch of sissies. It all starts in childhood with the fact that we're constantly wrapped up. Our parents mean well. They worry and only want what's best for us. They want us to be nice and warm and cuddly. But babies don't get cold that easily. They still have enough brown fat.

So what in the world is brown fat? Since there are now countless articles on this topic, I'll only focus on the essentials here. Our bodies contain brown fat, white fat and beige fat (this type is still the least researched). We are all familiar with white fat. People who have a bit too much of it have those famous *love handles*. ☺

Among other things, brown fat is activated when we are exposed to temperatures below 60 degrees Fahrenheit (16°Celsius). This means that it begins to burn white fat, thus generating heat in our body.

Babies have a lot of brown fat, which keeps them from feeling cold. If we keep wrapping our babies up, here's what happens: we already know that the body breaks down everything that we no longer need or use (think of the muscle example). So brown fat is broken down because we simply don't need it if we are constantly wrapped up in warm clothes.

By the time we grow up, we have almost no brown fat left and get cold easily. Of course, there are exceptions:

a) If you have enough white fat, it acts as insulation.

b) If you have enough muscle—the body's power plant—heat is naturally produced too.

c) If you have a hormone-related condition occurring, such as menopause, etc., you don't get cold easily.

But back to the brown fat. If we weren't wrapped up so much as children, we would preserve our brown fat and as adults, would be able to deal much better with the cold.

I have to say, we definitely lose brown fat over the course of our lives, but how much we keep largely depends on how often we use it.

If you observe children on a playground, you'll clearly see that they are not cold. The children are playing, and the parents are yelling: "Put on your jacket. It's cold! You're going to get sick!" While the kids are yelling back: "But I'm not cold!" This conversation goes back and forth for a few minutes until the children finally get a sweater, vest or jacket pushed over their head.

Now, if you are one of those parents reading this who is thinking: "OK, but they really would catch a cold." Let me tell you: that's not true. They don't catch a cold because they're not wearing enough, but because they already have some kind of illness lying dormant that is then triggered more easily. It's the same with adults. Just because you go out with your hair wet doesn't mean you'll catch a cold, but yes, we lose a lot of heat through our heads, so your core body temperature will drop. If, at the same time, you have an illness lying dormant, it is more likely to flare up. This has to do with the fact that the immune system is briefly suppressed by the cold (the open window effect).

Has Sonja *really* lost her mind now? So is the cold bad or not? No, of course not. On the contrary, the immune system gets a great boost! Let's go back to the muscles because everyone can understand that example. If you train a muscle, it gains mass. Exercising a muscle means exposing it to a bit of stress. For example, you put pressure on the muscle when you lift weights. In the regeneration phase, the muscle grows because it thinks the stress is over. If you consistently train your biceps with four-pound dumbbells, at some point, your muscles will have adapted to that weight so well that you can train for hours on end but never have sore biceps. The muscle will no longer grow either, which is why you have to keep increasing the weight you lift when you train.

So how does it work with the cold? It's very similar, but there are some differences. 😊 You strengthen (train) your immune system by repeatedly exposing it to short bouts of cold. It's like the famous Kneipp therapy. Maybe you've heard of *kniepping*, or water treading?

You expose your body to brief stress, something like a cold shower or a short cold bath, and just like when training your muscles, your immune system gets a boost through the cold bath.

If you would like an in-depth look at this and are interested in knowing which blood cells are involved in the process, I recommend the book *The Healing Power of the Cold* by Dr. Josephine Worseck. She is a molecular biologist and can explain to you in great detail what goes on in your body when you step into the cold. For my book, the biological details are not important; what matters is that you understand that you can actually strengthen your immune system through cold therapy.

By the way, you can not only strengthen your immune system, but also alleviate many symptoms of illness, such as pain associated with rheumatism or various autoimmune diseases. Cold showers or baths are also wonderful forms of therapy for depression and burnout.

There are a number of other benefits of the cold here, such allergy relief, anti-inflammatory effects, improvement of general well-being, increased vitality, and more.

But once again, as with everything else:

Don't take my word for it; try it out.

8.3. Implementation into everyday life

So how does one implement regular cold therapy using the TeLaWi method into everyday life?

And what does TeLaWi mean again? It stands for *teilen, langsam, wiederholen* [divide, slow down, repeat]. That is the BEST way to change your habits.

If you are highly sensitive to the cold, start with very small steps. At the end of your shower, take the shower head in your hand, point the nozzle away from your body and turn the temperature *a little cooler*. Then let the water run across your feet or calves for a few seconds and notice how it feels on your body. Once you've done that, get out of the shower and go about your business as usual. 😊

That's all you have to do to get started. You can increase the experience each time you shower. There are three ways to do this:

1. Turn the water a little colder each time.
2. Let the water run across part of your body a little longer each time.
3. Involve more and more body parts, very slowly from the bottom up.

When I explain this at my workshops, I often get the question: "How long will it take before I can immerse my whole body in the cold water?"

That question always makes me smile, because each time I hear it, I'm reminded of how much we want to overthink things and have a plan. We always want to know where and how and for how long...

But it doesn't work that way with the cold; you have to listen to your body. Tune in to what feels good to you, and how long it feels good to you. Please stop trying to complete the cold shower assignment with your head.

By the way, you *can* actually use your head to complete it, just like with the ice bath. You make up your mind to do it, then you tough it out with all the stubbornness you can muster.

People who take that approach are also the ones who put their heads through the wall on a daily basis, instead of just looking for the door in the wall. They are often stubborn people, especially at work. They think they HAVE to do this now or it means they are weak. They need the reassurance for a self-confidence boost; heaven forbid anyone would think they are *warm shower* wimps.

That's an easy one to read in the faces of the people sitting in the ice bath. I'm able to read so much from people's faces in the ice bath that it almost frightens me how much I learn about them. 😊 For me it has become a real *reading*, as if text is written across their foreheads.

If that describes you, please don't do it that way. You'll clearly miss the point of cold therapy and mind management. You are only proving again how determined you can be when you want to be... which basically (what a nice word 🙂) is good, but you are not operating in trust. That's why it drains your energy. You put your head through the wall day after day in the cold shower. You want to prove to the world that you can do it, even though you're all by yourself in the shower. So... relax. Nobody is watching. 🙂

If you prefer not to be stuck in your head or to force yourself, but you still want to quickly master the ice cold shower, here's a tip:

Commitment. Trust.

If you can do that, you'll master it the very first time. If you're determined to take a very cold shower, you trust in yourself and in your body and just let *it* happen, you can even do it today, without convulsing, without forcing yourself, without needing to prove anything to anyone.

Is it easy? No! But it is easy once you understand it and internalize it. Try out Commitment! Action! and Trust! in as many situations as you can in your life, and it will become easier and easier for you to apply it in difficult situations.

And practice the TeLaWi method. Take your time; you don't have to be perfect tomorrow. Forget our hectic world, which has been giving us the message for the past few decades that everything has to happen immediately and without delay. Give yourself time, give your body time and enjoy the ride. 😊

So now... put down the book and jump in the (cold) shower!

9. Your Commitment and the Reaction of Others

Now comes the very best part of commitment and trust! Let's call this the CT method. And the best thing about it is the reactions of other people, their reactions to the situation and to you.

If you are really determined, you will save yourself a lot of trouble. Because other people will get a very strong sense of your determination. That doesn't mean that they'll jump on board with you and be super excited about what you're doing or how you react, but at least they'll leave you alone. They will sense how serious you are and will no longer challenge it.

Feel free to try that out. It doesn't matter if you're a manager or a parent. This also works wonderfully for dog and cat owners. If you say something calmly but firmly in a way that shows everyone that there is absolutely no doubt that you mean business, the others will not contradict you. It might sound strange to you, but not even cats *do their own thing*. They, too, listen to what you say. 😊

But as soon as you say something half-heartedly; as soon as the other person has the feeling that there might be another possibility, you will encounter resistance.

But don't take my word for it; try it out.

Let's take a specific example from the family. You want your child to put their plate in the dishwasher after they eat. I have a daughter of my own, and had three patchwork kids, so I know exactly what I'm talking about here. 😊

It usually goes like this:
The parent: please put your plate in the dishwasher after dinner.
Child: yeah, yeah.
Parent: I'm serious.
Child: yeah, yeah, I will.

After dinner, of course, nothing happens. To keep up appearances, the child might take the plate into the kitchen; that's a good start after all.

So what do we do next? We notice it, maybe even after some time has passed. We let out a big sigh, get annoyed and put away the plate ourselves. Or we look at the child and say: "You're in the kitchen anyway; go ahead and put the plate straight into the dishwasher." Which one of these excuses sound familiar to you? I've heard them all:

1. I can't now; I have homework.

2. The dishes in the dishwasher are clean. It needs to be emptied first.
3. I can't find a spot; it's already so full.
4. Nah, I don't want to. Can't you do it?
5. Yeah, yeah, I'll do it later (but nothing happens and the child leaves).

So what do we do now? We either start flinching, yelling or slamming stuff around. Or we just do it ourselves, because after all, if the kid is doing their homework without being asked, we should support them in that. ☺ Or we do it ourselves, because after all, the dishwasher does have to be emptied first. Often you prefer to do it yourself because it gets done right; otherwise, you'll just have to redo it later. If you are a parent, you know exactly what I'm talking about. ☺

What can we do differently? Try Commitment!

You don't take a friendly tone, but you don't take an unfriendly one either... you say in a neutral, deep, firm, and determined voice: "After dinner, everyone puts their plate in the dishwasher. No exceptions and no excuses." And you say this while looking your kids straight in the eye.

The first time you try this, you'll get some surprised looks because it's new, and they'll want to test out how serious you are. You'll hear the same excuses you heard before. But this time you'll react differently. You'll answer every argument in a calm, deep, firm voice:

Child 1: I can't now; I have homework.

You: you can do your homework once you've put your plate in the dishwasher. Go do that now (don't raise your voice, don't get nervous, just deliver in a calm, determined voice).

Child 2: the dishes in the dishwasher are clean. It needs to be emptied first.

You: that's true! Good eye! You can start that right away.

Child 3: I can't find a spot; it's already so full.

You: I'm sure you can find a spot for your plate. Look a bit harder!

Child 4: nah, I don't want to. Can't you do it?

You: no, you need to do it... now.

Child 5: yeah, yeah, I will (but nothing happens and the child starts to leave).

You: stop right there! You know what you need to do. Go put your plate in the dishwasher... now.

Always stay calm, and be decisive. You'll be surprised what becomes possible. But you have to really be committed. You can't accept any excuses. You have to be very sure of yourself and confident that you will pull it off this time. Once you've done this a few times, you'll never have to say it again. Your kids will know that when you get that tone, you mean business! 😉

But don't take my word for it; try it out.

Oh right, and one more very important point: once that starts working, don't get on a grin on your face and let them see how satisfied you are. Simply say thank you and go into another room. There you can giggle and grin until the cows come home. 😊

This approach also applies to your dreams, goals and vision. That is, if you choose to share them with someone, because you feel like you have to. If you do, then show so much resolve that the other person won't even get the idea to disagree with you in the first place. It's better not to talk very much about your goals at all; that way, you are definitely on the safe side. I won't say much about the topic of who to talk to and who not to talk to, because I cover it in detail in my first book in the chapter on energy vampires.

10. Practical Examples of Determination, Action and Trust

10.1. Example 1 – Trust yourself

Here, I'd like to share the example of the five-time ice swimming world champion, Claudia Müller. In January 2020, she swam the famous Ice Mile. Swimming the Ice Mile means that she swam the mile-long stretch of water at temperatures below 40 degrees Fahrenheit (5°Celsius). She was only the second woman in Austria to complete it. The first was Yasmine Pliessnig, a magnificent swimmer, with whom I am completing the first ice swimming workshops in Austria. 

But back to Claudia Müller, a fascinating woman as well. I have had the privilege of interviewing her several times and asking her questions about her body and mindset. The topic of the Ice Mile came up once, and she told me that she speaks to her body. Her body speaks back, by the way, continuously giving her signals. But she says that she is in charge, which brings us back to the topic of mind over body and of commitment and trust.

She practiced a lot for the Ice Mile, and was absolutely determined to make it. That's the part where she committed to something with her whole heart and took control of her body. She explained that she spoke to her body and as she entered the water, she said: "Now you're here. It's time to swim."

Was she nervous? Sure she was! Very nervous, in fact, and tense because she was embarking on something completely unknown. Shortly before the start, a trainer said to the participants: "You can all swim the half mile, but past that point, it's uncharted territory to you all."

I'm sure you have no idea what kind of stress the Ice Mile puts on the body, but I promise you, it is damn tough. The farthest I have swum in icy water is 0.12 miles (200 meter), and I have to admit that my ambition to complete the full mile is pretty limited. 🙂 Haha.

You have to have a doctor and a rescue team on site, as well as officials from the Ice Swimming Association who officiate the Ice Mile, and much more. Many who start the Ice Mile have to stop because at some point it becomes too dangerous. But not Claudia; she persevered, kept her pace and spoke to herself and her body.

After completing the Ice Mile, she was only halfway out of the dark. Why? Because her body then had to warm back up, and that's not as easy as it sounds. So how did Claudia Müller do that? She said to her body after the

Ice Mile: "OK, I have swum the Ice Mile and now it's your turn to warm back up." With that sentence, she went completely into a state of trust and turned off her mind. The body did what it thought was right and Claudia left it alone to do so.

I love that story because it expresses exactly the message I would like to get across in this book:

Make a decision to do something, see it through and then just trust. Stop interfering with your mind; stop thinking. 😊

It's the same in an ice bath; it's the exact same principle. Or even in a cold shower... try it out!

10.2. Example 2 - Trust your body

This example is about Josef Kroh. Josef is 70 years old and has multiple sclerosis (MS). After hearing about how breathing work and ice baths have helped others with MS, I asked him in 2018 if he would like to give it a try. I wanted to know if what the Wim Hof community claims is really true. You see, I can still be quite skeptical too, which is why carrying out my own experiments is very important to me. 😊

I explained to him what it was about, showed him the breathing technique and then led him into the ice bath. It was nice to watch Josef because his focus wasn't on the cold temperature of the ice bath, but on the effect that it had on his illness. He was able to commit to the bath and enter a state of trust. He closed his eyes and relaxed:

Photo: Josef Flandorfer

He did an excellent job, and was even reluctant to get out because he could tell how much good it was doing him. And what he told me a week later exceeded even my expectations. He said he was eager to take another ice bath because he had been free from pain for almost a week.

Do you realize what it means for an MS patient to be pain-free for a week? He was used to enduring pain 24 hours a day, 7 days a week. Not to mention the resting pain he experienced in bed at night. A good night's sleep was usually out of the question. He would often fall asleep during the day because he was deprived of sleep at night.

But the ice bath had put an end to that. A week's worth of improved quality of life, a week of better sleep, a week of more energy. Josef Kroh is now one of my regular ice bathers.

10.3. Example 3 - Trust your gut

In this example, we will move away from the subject of the cold and toward our gut feeling. But we'll stick with trust.

It's May 14, 2020. My husband has decided to buy a grill from a wholesaler. Today, they go on sale for 25% off. He gets up in the morning and asks me to go with him. I'm a little annoyed because I had other plans, but OK, I can be flexible. ☺ He starts questioning whether he should buy the grill or not. Since I don't care at all, I tell him it's his decision to make. He's pacing the room, when I finally say: "Stop thinking so much. What does your gut say? Sit down, take three deep breaths, ask yourself: 'Should I buy this grill?' and then see what comes next." And he actually heard an immediate *no*. His gut clearly said no.

Ten seconds later he says: "I'm tired of fooling around. Let's just go. I'm going to buy the grill." I think to myself: uh oh, if your gut says no and gets overruled by your head, that's never good, but whatever, let's go.

We arrive at the wholesaler and what do you know? It's sold out, even though we called the night before and made sure that it was still in stock. We had driven 50 miles (80 km) and spent 1.5 hours in the car for nothing. Well, it wasn't exactly for *nothing*, because we learned a couple lessons from it:

1. We don't trust ourselves and our intuition nearly enough.
2. We believe we have to solve everything with our heads.

And I had one more example for my book. 

My husband said it was important for him to go, because otherwise he would have always wondered if the grill had been there and if we would have bought it. In other words, it would have still been up in the air. To which I replied that we could also just trust our intuitions more, which would save us from driving 50 miles (80 km) and from wrestling with the question of *What if?*

And that is the most difficult thing in life... learning to trust! Learning to trust that everything is as it should be, to trust that we know what is best for us, to trust our intuition.

If you ever find yourself in a situation like that, where you don't know what to do, then sit down, take a few deep breaths (at least three), ask the question you want answered and I promise you, you'll get an answer right away.

Some people literally hear a voice. I don't hear a voice, but a thought comes right away. And it's precisely that FIRST thought, the first voice or the first feeling that is the right one. If you hear or feel something else three seconds later, forget it... your head is back in the game.

Commitment! Trust!

And then it's about committing to that first thought and trusting it. Trust that your first instinct is the right one. But of course, you can test anything out: do exactly the opposite of what you heard or felt, and see what happens. I promise you there will be a hitch and it would have been better the other way around.

But as I always say: don't take my word for it; try it out.

11. Summary and Tips

RealTalk's second online event took place on June 20, 2020. Incidentally, I can recommend RealTalk to anyone who is interested in personal development. A few young, committed, wonderful people have come together with the goal of making personal development cool again. And you can imagine, I love anything that is *cool*! 😊

It is usually a live event, and it will be again in the future. There are three speakers at each event, who share their experiences. They speak about life changes, defeats, success and failure. It's a fantastic format!

On June 20 (online this year because of our *special* circumstances), Matthias Strolz, Cathy Zimmermann and Philipp Maderthaner were featured. It was like each one of them was taking the words out of my mouth. But I'd like to just share a few points that are important for this book.

Cathy Zimmermann said this: "Surround yourself with people who are supportive." A good tip, but then came a question from a viewer (you could ask questions in the online chat): "How do I find people like that?"

I can answer that one for you here. There are just two things you have to do:

1. Be a supportive person yourself, help others (but don't let people take advantage of you; there's a difference!);

2. Be committed to what you do and you won't have to look for supportive people; they will suddenly pop up in your life. Remember Erich and Kurt? Those are just two of the many wonderful people I have encountered.

Philipp Maderthaner finished with a brilliant talk and mentioned that not everything can be planned. Our ToDo lists are endless, but we still can't manage to check everything off. He went on to say: "Relax; you can't always get everything done."

What Philipp means here with "relax" is the same thing as me telling you to "trust." Make out your ToDo list, no problem, but don't give yourself a hard time if there isn't a check mark beside every ToDo at the end of the day. Trust that today, you will get today's most important tasks done, and that you will get to the other things later. You will even notice that some of them resolve themselves or are simply no longer important.

Set goals for yourself; goals are great and very important, BUT—and here it comes—don't get in the way of your own goals. Be disciplined and work on them every day, but stop demanding IRON discipline from yourself.

Not sure what I mean?

Commitment! Trust!

Work on your goals each and every day; above all, work on your mindset each and every day. Reprogram your mind, but immediately after you do, enter into a state of trust, take a deep breath and relax. You did everything you could today, so give yourself a pat on the back.

11.1. Clarifying action, commitment and trust

In this summary, I would like to repeat something that I have already written, because it is extremely important and should not be misunderstood under any circumstances.

There are people who think they just have to have the right amount of determination, then they can sit on the couch and light some incense, and everything will gravitate their way.

I already touched on this in the example of turning on the lights. If you are determined that you want to turn on the lights, but you don't do it, and sit on the couch instead, nothing will happen.

But if you are determined to turn on the lights and you flip the switch, and trust that it will work, then the lights will come on.

Yes, you have to take action, but you don't have to know exactly how to reach your goal. Your goal can even change and can deviate from what you originally wanted.

If you are working toward a new goal, then it will be a path you've never taken before. Trust will help you along, but you have to get started. If you can't get past your starting position, you won't reach your goal.

That's why it's so important to me to repeat this again here, because quite a few people, triggered by the esoteric and energetic wave that is flooding our world, believe that they don't have to do anything to be happy, healthy or successful.

I also believe that we create our own reality with our thoughts and words. I don't just believe it, I know it. I'm 100% sure because I've been experimenting with that for over 15 years. In order to create our own reality, we have to generate the right thoughts. How do we do that? By thinking them!

As we know, we are shaped by our environment and our surroundings. It is up to us to reprogram our minds if we want to live differently from those around us. And reprogramming means we have to take action.

And yes, you've read the words *have to* pretty often by now, but I think they are important. If you are one of those people who say: "I don't *have to* do anything," then knock yourself out. Go see how far that takes you. I am convinced that if you want to change your life, then you HAVE TO get going and do something. Your life is not going to change itself.

OK, so let's dive right in: what kind of life do you want? Start reprogramming your mind right now. Check out Section 11.3 for a tip on that.

11.2. The best way to use ToDo lists

If you want a specific tip on the best way to use ToDo lists, then listen up (all you overthinkers in particular):

We usually make our ToDo lists and go through checking things off. At the end of the day, we look at our list and first notice what we didn't get done. This leaves us feeling frustrated and disappointed. Look at all those unchecked items.

Take a calendar and divide the day into two columns. In the first column, write exactly ONE task that you absolutely want to, or have to, get done today. Commit yourself to it; it's a must, so no excuses!

In the other column write your other ToDos. Then start completing the task in the left column. Check it off. You've completed your *must* for the day. Congratulations. Anything else you can check off in the right column is a bonus.

Celebrate every item you manage to check off, and at the end of the day, take a look at what you've accomplished. You will see that you have completed your *must* (left column) and AS A BONUS, you've checked some things off in the right column. You'll feel proud and motivated. 😊

11.3. Goalify – An app to keep you on track

There are several ways to stick to your goals, change your habits or reprogram yourself or your beliefs. I would like to introduce you to a tool that works great both on your cell phone and your PC: Goalify.

Goalify is an app where you can enter and check off your daily goals. It intuitively learns when you accomplish your goals each day and reminds you so that you don't forget about them.

The app is free of charge for up to three goals, so you can download it and give it a try. 😊

You enter a daily ToDo, such as reciting the following sentence: "I'm good enough." You tell the app how often you would like to meet this goal, for example, once a day for five days a week. You then check it off every day and TeLaWi, you'll change the way you think about yourself.

Why the app? Can't I do that on my own? Sure you can, but who will remind you? 😉 My experience with countless people is that we need reminders. Our everyday lives are often so stressful that we forget even the simplest things, like reciting a sentence.

All you need to complete this task is about three seconds. So don't tell me that you don't have the time.

If you are someone who would like to be persistent with the Wim Hof breathing, go to the top left of the Goalify app (the three little lines), then tap on Connect and enter the code: QQL 7UR 45K.

And you're automatically part of the Wim Hof Breathers group, where you will find motivation through positive peer pressure. And don't worry, the others taking the challenge won't see any of your data; no telephone number, nothing at all, just the name you enter (usually your first name only).

Every now and then, my customers tell me that it annoys them when Goalify pops up and says they should do something. You know what I think? That is precisely why you have the app, because you won't think to do it on your own! Complete your task and it won't pop up anymore. It's that simple. 😊

Don't go overboard at first. You can also take on one of the preset challenges.

So why am I pushing Goalify here? This is not an advertising platform; I just want to offer you a tool that will help you stay on track. You learned about the TeLaWi method, and I am asked again and again how to stick with it, how not to forget. This is a great tool for that.

But don't take my word for it; try it out.

12. The Big Goal: a Happier and Healthier Life

Don't look for quick success and fast money. Don't look at all! Find it! Find happiness, joy and health, and the rest will come on its own. I really mean that.

The goal is not to be successful without happiness. Being successful AND happy AND healthy; that's the goal, at least it's my goal. In my experience, and I have plenty of it by now, that is (most) everyone's goal.

Feel free to ditch the word *successful* if it sounds too materialistic to you. If you are happy and healthy, you are already a success.

Success means something different for everyone. In our society, it's often associated with having a lot of money. I think that's good. Because only those who have a lot of money can give away a lot of money. Now there are people who demonize money because they believe it's *bad*, and only brings bad luck. If you are one of those people, then money will indeed bring you bad luck. Your thoughts create your reality.

For me, money is something positive because I can use it to help other people, because it gives me a nice quality of life and because I can ensure that others have the same. How do you expect to donate money if you don't have any money? How do you expect to support others financially without money?

I earn my living with individual coaching, workshops and seminars. But I also give free workshops, for example, for the disabled, and I give free individual coaching sessions to people who are absolutely committed, want to take action but don't know how, and cannot afford my fees.

But I can only offer free services because I earn money with my other coaching sessions and seminars. What I mean is that when you have something, you can give something, in every sense.

If you have nothing to eat, how are you going to give away food? If you have no knowledge, how are you going to pass on knowledge? If you don't have money, how are you going to give away money? If you don't love yourself, and you don't carry love within your heart, how are you going to give someone love?

I am convinced that giving is a basic human need. But to be able to give, you must first have something to give, regardless of whether it is knowledge, money or love.

Think about that: what would YOU like to give others? Then you need to first stockpile whatever it is you want to give. Once you have it, you can give it and bring other people joy. Be a role model for others.

Even though some things in this book may sound strange to you, like all the stuff about *The Force* watching over us and speaking to us through synchronicities, I hope that you will give it all a chance.

Find out for yourself whether what I am writing here is true or not. As always: don't take my word for it; try it out.

Get going!

Commitment! Trust!

Action!

Keep on Cooling.

Sonja Flandorfer,
Austria's "Coolest" Lady

Book Tips

I really have a lot of good books to recommend. I keep adding to my list of favorite books.

There are books about our brain, our thinking, our behavior, and about cold therapy and mind management.

Since I can't always expand the list in this book, please have a look at my website: www.keep-on-cooling.com. There is a menu item there called "Buchertipps" (Book Tips).

I have mentioned some of them in this book, but you can still find quite a lot of very interesting literature on my website.

Glücklich für immer? So a Schaß!

And since I referred to it so much in this book, here is my previous book on Mind Management:

Available just in German

Claudia Müller, 5xGold

This book is about the life of five-time world champion Claudia Müller. From chronic hip problems to the World Cup.

Available just in German

Acknowledgments

A big THANK YOU goes out to:

Josef Flandorfer, my husband, for constantly backing up my bizarre ideas. Thank you.

Brigitte Freystetter, my mother. She might not always understand me, but in the end, she always stands behind me and is there when I need her. Thank you.

Tatjana Marina Kubera, my daughter. I've managed to escape the role of the embarrassing mother who is different from the other mothers, and have now become the super cool mom. And of course, she is different from the others, too. 😊 Thank you.

Alexandra Kleyhons; I have mentioned her several times in this book. She continues to support and inspire me. Thank you.

Prof. Dr. Manfred Winterheller, for your inspiration starting in November 2015 and before that, with the CDs. Thank you for showing me how to trust and how to communicate with *The Force*. Thank you.

Wim Hof, for your vision and your authenticity. Thank you for your zest for life and for showing me how happiness works. How to be happy in the cold, how to trust and how to love.

My friends Sabine Werther and Kurt and Gerda Strametz for your support, for lending me a hand and most of all, for understanding me. That means so much.

Herbert Kalser for editing and proofreading the german version of the book. Thank you very much, Herbert.

Cynthia Pecking for translating the book into English. Thanks a lot, Cynthia.

Annex

With Keep on Cooling, you'll discover cold therapy and mind management.

Photo: Sabine Werther

**Strengthen your mind through
concentration and by turning
your focus inward.**

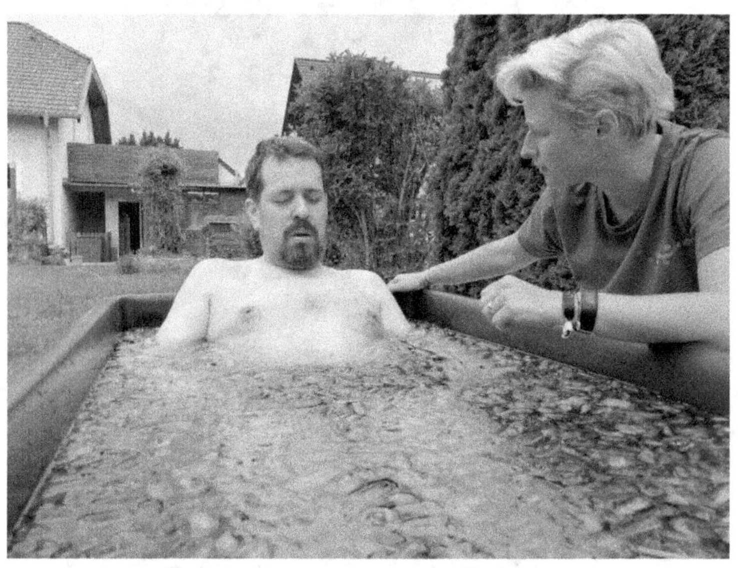

Photo: Josef Flandorfer

**Feel for yourself how you can have
control over your body,
by hiking with us in nothing
but shoes and shorts.**

Photo: Kurt Strametz

Get to know the feeling of the group. Support each other and draw the strength you need from the others.

Photo: 888lifechanger.com

**And have a blast
in the cold
with all that you've learned.**

Photo: Kurt Strametz

This is Claudia Müller, the five-time world champion in ice swimming at one of my weekend workshops.